Almos[...] [...]ste of
choco[...]s, life
revolve[...][...]ring,
and cr[...] [...]ymp-
toms of chocolate addiction include:

- CRAVING CHOCOLATE FREQUENTLY

- EATING LARGE AMOUNTS OF
  CHOCOLATE ALL AT ONCE

- FEELING OUT OF CONTROL
  WHEN EATING CHOCOLATE

- ...AND FEELING GUILTY
  AND ANGRY AFTERWARDS

- DEPENDING ON CHOCOLATE FOR A
  "BOOST" WHEN YOU'RE DEPRESSED

- TURNING TO CHOCOLATE FOR COMFORT

- EXPERIENCING A CHOCOLATE "HIGH"
  THAT'S SIMILAR TO SEXUAL AROUSAL

- ASSOCIATING FOND CHILDHOOD
  MEMORIES WITH CHOCOLATE.

THE CHOCOHOLIC'S DREAM DIET

tells you everything you need to know if you are or think
you may be a chocolate addict—from understanding
your physical cravings to finding satisfaction by incorpo-
rating chocolate into your diet within safe and nutrition-
ally sound guidelines. At last, it's possible to control
your weight—without giving up the taste you love!

The Chocoholic's Dream Diet

DOREEN L. VIRTUE, M.A.

BANTAM BOOKS
New York • Toronto • London • Sydney • Auckland

NOTE

The information contained in this book is intended to complement, not substitute for, the advice of your own physician, with whom you should consult about your individual needs. You should always consult with your own physician before starting any medical treatment or diet.

THE CHOCOHOLIC'S DREAM DIET

A Bantam Book / October 1990

ISBN 0-553-28443-6

Published simultaneously in the United States and Canada

Bantam Books are published by Bantam Books, a division of
Bantam Doubleday Dell Publishing Group, Inc. Its trademark,
consisting of the words "Bantam Books" and the portrayal of
a rooster, is Registered in U.S. Patent and Trademark Office
and in other countries. Marca Registrada. Bantam Books,
666 Fifth Avenue, New York, New York 10103.

PRINTED IN THE UNITED STATES OF AMERICA

OPM   0 9 8 7 6 5 4 3 2 1

Contents

I

Chocoholics

1

Chocoholics

Have you ever said to yourself, "I could lose weight if it wasn't for all the chocolate candy and ice cream I eat"? If so, then you're going to *love* this diet!

This is the first book to seriously study the love of, and the addiction to, chocolate. It is also the first book you'll read that will give you solutions and guidance. You'll learn why chocolate has such a powerful hold over your appetite. But, best of all, you'll learn how to lose weight *and* reduce the fat, cholesterol, and sodium in your diet without sacrificing chocolate!

The Chocoholic's Dream Diet includes balanced daily servings of chocolate goodies ... things like M & M's, sugar-free chocolate ice cream, and Oreo cookies. By following this healthy, delicious diet, you'll learn how to enjoy chocolate in moderation. You'll even learn step-by-step methods for preparing your own chocolate treats, many of them sugar free.

For a long time, chocoholics have been the subject of bad jokes and viewed with suspicion. "That's just an excuse to eat a lot of candy bars," nonchocoholics contend. "Just use your willpower and eat only one chocolate," we're told over and over again.

But that can be like telling an alcoholic to drink just one beer! For many chocoholics, there's no such thing as *one* piece of See's candy, or *one* Hershey's kiss. I know, from firsthand experience, what it's like to be a chocoholic and to crave chocolate uncontrollably. And as a psychotherapist specializing in treating food addictions, I've helped myself and hundreds of other chocoholics learn how to fit chocolate into their weight-loss plans.

Most people know whether they're chocoholics or not. Some even proudly announce their chocoholism on bumper stickers or T-shirts. But just in case you're not sure, or if you don't know to what *degree* your chocoholism has evolved, please take this test:

Are You a Chocoholic?

True or false:

1. I frequently crave chocolate.
2. My favorite food has chocolate in it.
3. At times, I go on chocolate binges and eat an entire carton of chocolate ice cream, a bag of chocolate cookies, most of a chocolate cake, or a lot of chocolate candy.
4. True or false for women: I crave chocolate right before my menstrual cycle.
5. It seems I always eat more chocolate in the winter, and I gain weight during the cold months as a result.
6. I have gone to great lengths to get my favorite chocolate treat (e.g., driven several miles out of my way, spent money I didn't have, etc.).
7. I mostly eat chocolate treats when others aren't around, and I even hide the chocolate's empty packaging so others won't know what I've eaten.
8. After I eat chocolate, I feel guilty and angry at myself.
9. Just the sight or smell of chocolate is enough to make me want it.

10. I think I'm a hopeless romantic; I fall in love easily, and I can't get enough of romantic movies or books.

11. The best thing about chocolate is its taste.

12. If I were stranded on a deserted isle, I'd definitely want chocolate to be one of the supplies in my survival pack.

13. Life without chocolate wouldn't be much fun.

14. The last time I broke with a lover, I was depressed for days.

15. It really seems like I want chocolate most during the holidays, such as Halloween, Christmas, Easter, or Passover.

16. Every time I have a bite of chocolate, I lose total control of my appetite and I want to eat every bit of chocolate I can get my hands on.

17. I've noticed that I feel really good when I'm eating chocolate. It's like a natural high to eat it.

18. Others have kidded me or commented that I seem to like chocolate more than "normal" people do.

19. Sometimes I use chocolate as a pick-me-up when I'm feeling tired or depressed.

20. I have fond childhood memories surrounding the eating of chocolate.

21. Speaking of childhood, as a kid I used to hide when I ate chocolate. I never let my parents or siblings know when I was eating chocolate treats.

22. It seems I'm always able to keep the weight off until the fall holidays from Halloween until New Year's. There's just so much chocolate being passed around during those holidays that I always gain weight.

23. To me, the more chocolate flavor, the better, I'll always opt for "double chocolate" ice cream

instead of light milk chocolate or (yech!) plain vanilla.

24. I always think of chocolate as being "bad" food— bad for my weight, bad for my health—but so good tasting that I allow myself to be "naughty" and eat some.

25. I can't stand the taste of carob. To me, it's fake chocolate.

26. When my mom used to ask me what flavor cake I'd like for my birthday, I'd *always* ask for chocolate cake with chocolate frosting.

27. I like chocolate more than anyone else in my family does.

28. I go on chocolate "kicks"; that is, I'll like a certain type of chocolate and eat only that type until I get sick of it. Then I'll like a different type of chocolate until I get sick of that kind.

29. I only seem to binge on chocolate when it contains refined sugar, such as a candy bar, cake, or ice cream. I don't feel like overeating when I have sugar-free chocolate candy, ice cream, or frozen yogurt.

30. After an argument with my spouse or lover, I usually crave or eat chocolate.

31. I feel happy and excited right before I'm about to eat my favorite chocolate treat.

32. If others knew how much chocolate I really ate, I'd feel embarrassed—even humiliated.

33. To me, chocolate is a sensual food. I've noticed that chocolate's texture and taste arouse my sexual desires.

34. When I go to the movies, I'd rather eat chocolate candy instead of popcorn.

35. If my lover brought me home my very favorite chocolate treat (frozen yogurt, candy, cookies, etc.), I couldn't help but view it as an act of love.

Scoring Information

Count the number of "true" answers, and match the number with the scoring below:

0 to 10
You may enjoy an occasional chocolate, but you're not a chocoholic. You can take chocolate or leave it, and when ordering an ice cream cone or frozen yogurt, you often order vanilla or fruit flavors. When you eat sweets, it's frequently the hard-candy or pastry variety. In other words, chocolate is really no big deal to you. You may know or love a chocoholic, however, and to you, the whole subject of chocoholism is a mystery or a joke.

11 to 20
You're a "borderline chocoholic"—you like chocolate a lot, but your whole life doesn't revolve around it. Instead, you've probably noticed that chocolate is something you enjoy at regular intervals, perhaps if someone has happened to bring some to work or your house. You wouldn't turn it down if it were offered to you, but you wouldn't go out of your way to get it, either.

You've eaten your share of chocolate candy and cakes, and when dieting, you've sworn off of all sweets and desserts. But like others who are fond of chocolate, you've found that chocolate—when others offer it to you—has been the downfall of many of your weight-loss attempts.

21 to 29
You are definitely a chocoholic and you know it. You prefer chocolate to any other flavor, and you wouldn't

dream of ordering a vanilla ice-cream cone. You've driven across town to get your favorite chocolate treat, even when you're short on time or money. You've eaten chocolate to celebrate good times, as well as to comfort yourself during the bad times.

At times, you've felt out of control around chocolate, like an alcoholic around alcohol, and there have been many times when you've felt you couldn't stop eating the chocolate candies or cookies in front of you. You know you're addicted, at least psychologically, to chocolate, and you loathe diets because they make you give up your favorite food.

30 to 35
You're an "ultimate chocoholic"—a hard-core addict who lives for the taste and smell of chocolate. You crave and eat chocolate every day, if not several times a day. You plan your day so that you'll have time to stop off at the store or the ice-cream/frozen-yogurt shop to get your favorite chocolate treat.

Others probably kid you about your chocolate obsession, but you don't care—at least not enough to ever stop eating chocolate. In the past, you've sworn off chocolate, but you really think it's a losing battle and that you're a hopelessly incurable chocoholic.

Now that you've analyzed the intensity of your chocoholism, it's important to determine what *style* of chocoholism you tend toward. My research, conducted at my eating disorder clinics in Southern California and through interviews with more than three hundred chocoholics across America, combined with medical research on the role food plays in mental and physical health, shows that people overeat chocolate in different ways and for different reasons.

The first step in gaining control over your chocolate appetite is to find out what type of chocoholic you are, because your weight-loss program needs to be custom-tailored to fit your personality and behavior patterns. I can't emphasize this enough: Not all chocoholics are alike!

To find your style, please review the answers you gave on the true/false questions and match them with the following style guide.

If you answered "true" to three or more of these questions: 10, 14, 30, 33, 35, then you are a "Chocolate Lover." A Chocolate Lover is someone who has a high need for romance and love. The Lover binges on the good feelings produced by eating chocolate, feelings aroused by the chemicals contained in chocolate.

If you answered "true" to three or more of these questions: 4, 5, 15, 22, 26, then you are a "Situational Chocoholic." There are three general subcategories of Situational Chocoholics:

1. The woman who craves chocolate right before her menstrual cycle because of hormonal fluctuations.
2. The person who desires chocolate only during the cold winter months because of seasonally influenced depression.
3. The person who just wants chocolate when it's around, especially during the chocolate-filled holidays, Easter, Passover, Halloween, Valentine's Day, Hanukkah, and Christmas.

If you answered "true" to three or more of these questions: 3, 6, 16, 28, 29, then you are a "Chocolate Binger." This person literally cannot have one bite of chocolate without going into an all-out eating binge. Some Bingers only lose control with chocolate containing refined sugar, other Bingers overeat certain *types* of chocolate treats, such as ice cream or cake.

If you answered "true" to three or more of these questions: 9, 13, 17, 19, 31, then you are a "Euphoric Chocoholic." The Euphoric Chocoholic experiences complete and utter bliss when eating chocolate. This person usually describes eating chocolate as a "completely perfect experience," and the Euphoric would be hard-pressed to tell you which aspect of chocolate is more important: the taste, smell, or texture. All in all, the Euphoric feels a definite high from eating chocolate.

If you answered "true" to three or more of these questions: 7, 8, 21, 24, 32, then you are a "Closet Chocoholic." This person usually feels very guilty about eating anything labeled "fattening"—which includes chocolate. The Closet often hides while eating a favorite chocolate treat. He or she may hide candy bar wrappers in a purse or car, or wait for family members to go to sleep so that the chocolate cake or ice cream can be eaten alone.

In the pages that follow, you'll find a full chapter devoted to explaining each style. Many people will find that they are more than one style; some people are all five styles. If you are a combination of two or more styles, then follow the guidelines in the chapters that apply to your styles.

2

Sex, Romance, and Chocolate:
The Chocolate Lover

The link between chocolate and romance goes back to the days of courtship, when the gentleman caller brought his intended a heart-shaped box of chocolates. Together, they'd sit in the parlor, gaze into each other's eyes, and eat bonbons.

This scenario is no accident, however, because more and more research is revealing the powerful aphrodisiac qualities inherent in chocolate. Most people have heard by now that chocolate contains the same chemical that the brain creates when we are feeling the delicious emotions of romantic love and infatuation.

Remember feeling light-headed, excited, and tingly all over when you first fell in love? Remember how high you felt, how right with the world? (Maybe you're lucky enough to be feeling that way right now!) Those physical sensations which we call "falling in love" have a lot to do with phenylethylamine (pronounced: fen-el-eth-el-a-meen), the chemical your brain secretes when you're deeply, romantically attracted to someone. Chocolate contains phenylethylamine in exactly the same form as the brain produces. Therefore, when you eat chocolate, you're apt to feel an enveloping sensation of warmth, tingles, and excitement similar to being in love!

Certain people—the Chocolate Lovers—are especially attracted to these feelings, and this is the main reason they overeat chocolate. Studies conducted in 1987 by Margorie Schuman, Ph.D., a professor at California School of Professional Psychology, bears this out. Schuman studied people who described themselves as having the following personality traits:

- Likes to be dramatic and/or flamboyant (this includes a need to be the center of attention).
- Experiences frequent mood swings.
- Falls in love more easily than others.
- Tends to be devastated by romantic rejection.
- Very sensitive to the approval or disapproval of others.

She found that individuals with these characteristics often ate chocolate and other sweets to "medicate" or cover up feelings of depression, tension, and irritability.

My 28-year-old client Cathy fit this profile perfectly. An executive secretary who attended college in the evening, Cathy felt extremely insecure when social conversations didn't revolve around her accomplishments. She was constantly telling her friends about the "A" she'd received on a test or the report she'd finished for her boss. If the topic of discussion moved to another subject, Cathy would find some way to bring her friends' attention back on herself. Likewise, when she first came in for therapy, Cathy was reluctant to reveal anything less than flattering about herself to me, thinking I'd reject her if she were less than perfect.

Cathy's world also revolved around her constant short-lived infatuations, usually with men completely wrong for her. During the first six months of our therapy, Cathy was sure that ten different men were "Mr. Right." She'd talk briefly to a male student or a new client at work and, "boom"—Cathy was swept off her feet.

For instance, there was 23-year-old Rick, who lived with his mother while he studied philosophy part-time. Cathy was attracted to Rick's blazing green eyes and his lively classroom discussions about Søren Kierkegaard and existentialism. One day after class, she walked with him out to the parking lot and asked for his phone number. That was the beginning, and for the next three weeks, Cathy and Rick were inseparable—until the day Cathy called Rick and his mother answered the phone. When Rick's mom innocently explained that Rick was "out with his girlfriend, Monica," Cathy dropped out of Philosophy 101.

There were other men, all equally inappropriate and destructive to Cathy's self-esteem. Why would such a bright, attractive woman put herself in such demoralizing situations? What we discovered in therapy was that Cathy was addicted to her feelings of romantic love. The *object* of her affections, in other words, the *man*, wasn't that important. What did matter was that Cathy would constantly feel that delicious feeling of infatuation and everything that went along with it: the butterflies in the stomach, the lighthearted feeling, the excited anticipation.

In the midst of all this, Cathy's self-image would swing from grandiosity to utter dejection. This is how she described it after she'd been in therapy for two months: "Sometimes I feel like I'm the most powerful, beautiful, talented woman on earth. Like I could do anything, even own the whole world if I wanted to! I'd never admit those feelings to anyone else, because they'd think I was really stuck-up and wouldn't understand. But during those moments, I feel so high, so proud of who I am, and it's like nothing's gonna stop me from getting every one of my goals accomplished.

"Then something will happen, like my boss will find a mistake I did, or I'll break up with a boyfriend, and I suddenly feel like a world-class idiot. I'll get down on myself, saying things to myself like, 'You jerk! How dare you think you could ever graduate from college or get a promotion at work! You're just a stupid idiot.' Then I'll feel really depressed and I won't answer the phone or doorbell 'cause I won't want to talk to anyone. And I won't want them to see me, because when I get that way I feel so *ugly*."

During the times when Cathy felt, as she put it, "lower than a piece of dirt," she'd isolate herself from the outside world, close the curtains, and allow clutter and dirty dishes to pile up in her apartment. And she'd also binge on everything chocolate she could get her hands on: Haagen-Dazs chocolate ice cream, Oreo cookies, and even uncooked double-chocolate-chip cookie dough. Cathy would rationalize her eating by telling herself, "I deserve this," or "Who cares how much I weigh? I don't ever want to be with a man again!"

Therapy, for Cathy, consisted of helping her see how much power and control she was giving to others. In other words, she was allowing others to determine how she felt about herself. If someone complimented Cathy, or if she received an "A," Cathy felt great about herself. If, on the other hand, someone criticized or broke up with her, Cathy's self-esteem would plummet. When Cathy learned how to enjoy, but not depend on, others' compliments and praise, she stopped having the wide swings in self-image.

Cathy's case, and other Chocolate Lovers like her, remind me of the great quote, "Compliments are like perfume. They should be inhaled but not swallowed."

Of course compliments and praise feel good, *but when we rely on them to tell us how and who we are,* we give too much power to others.

Chocolate and Your "Sexual Metabolism"

The ultimate aphrodisiac, I suppose, would be a chocolate-covered oyster. Of course, that doesn't sound very appetizing, but it does bring up the subject of sex, and its relationship to chocolate.

Unfortunately and perhaps surprisingly, most Chocolate Lovers that I've treated or interviewed reported dissatisfaction with their sex life. As with my client Cathy, they would console their feelings of loneliness and depression about these unfulfilling relationships by eating chocolate. But by doing so, these Chocolate Lovers were also unwittingly *adding* to their sexual problems.

The majority of my sexually dissatisfied clients were disinterested in having physical relationships with their spouses or lovers. Most were also "autosexual," meaning they preferred to receive sexual gratification through masturbation instead of intercourse.

As an example, let me tell you about my client Samantha, a pretty 38-year-old supermarket cashier. Married for the second time four years before, Samantha told me she couldn't stand her husband to hold or kiss her. "It always starts out as a nice hug, but soon Rob wants me to take off his clothes and have sex with him," she complained. "It's easier just to stay away from him altogether, because I can't stand sex anymore."

Although Rob and Samantha had a romantic and sexually exciting first year of marriage, Samantha found herself losing interest in sex soon after they had their first child. During her pregnancy, Samantha had gained fifty pounds from eating a steady diet of chocolate ice cream and cheeseburgers, and was only able to lose twenty pounds after their daughter was born.

The weight gain had thrown Samantha for a loop— she'd never had a weight problem before! All of a sudden, Samantha felt matronly and ugly, and she didn't want Rob to look at her, let alone touch her. "It was like I had turned into my mother," Samantha remembered. "I saw myself as an old, fat woman with dimply cellulite on her thighs. And it's hard to be horny when you think you look like a cow. Rob always tells me my weight doesn't matter—he says there's more of me to love—but with this extra weight I just don't feel sexy anymore."

Samantha still eats chocolate every day, but she's switched from ice cream to frozen yogurt to save calories. Unfortunately, Samantha is choosing fattening versions of yogurt. A small or medium nonfat chocolate yogurt is one thing, but Samantha's favorite is a large low-fat chocolate yogurt with carob peanuts on top—a treat that adds almost four hundred fat-laden calories to her daily diet.

Another client, 31-year-old Christine, seemingly had the opposite sexual problem from Samantha. Christine had as insatiable an appetite for sex as she did for chocolate, and she could never get enough of either. She and her husband would have sex at least once a day during the week and several times during the weekend. And there's more: Christine also had a boyfriend with whom she slept two or three times a week.

Her preoccupation with sex was matched only by her obsession with chocolate. Christine was overweight in an extremely sexy, voluptuous Mae West sort of way, and because her factory job surrounded her with men, she never lacked for sexual partners. During therapy,

Christine complained that she felt controlled by her obsessions; she felt she had no choice but to have sex and eat candy bars. Even though Christine felt unhappy in her marriage, she didn't want to leave her husband because "the sex is so great." And even though she desperately wanted to lose forty pounds, she couldn't stay away from the candy vending machines because "chocolate tastes so great and makes me feel so good."

Both Samantha and Christine learned how their chocoholism was both a cause and an effect of their sexual problems. For Samantha, and other women and men disinterested in sex or physical contact, the abuse of chocolate and other stimulant foods (colas, coffee, tea, and sugared foods) can lead to tremendous amounts of tension and irritability. Many people abuse the theobromine and tyramine, the chief stimulant agents in chocolate which instantly raise blood pressure and make you feel like you're raring to go. They want energy, so they eat chocolate.

While the amount of caffeine in chocolate is relatively small compared to, say, a cup of coffee, this stimulant still contributes to a feeling of being "up" after you've eaten chocolate. Add to this the blood sugar boost from the refined sugar, and it's easy to see why chocoholics use this food like a drug to get them going when they feel sluggish.

Unfortunately, after eating these pep foods all day long, it's difficult to unwind. Sexual enjoyment depends on being able to relax and enjoy the sensations of your body, as well as your partner's. If, however, you're uptight, tense, and irritable, you're more likely to get into an argument than a romantic mood. This is why so many of my chocoholics, like Samantha, become autosexual; they can only relax when having sex by themselves.

Eating stimulant foods for energy creates a cycle of dependency, as well. Let me explain: If you pump yourself up with chocolate, caffeine, and sugar all day long, you'll have to ingest a downer, or depressant, in the evening in order to slow down and get some sleep. Many people turn to alcohol or soothing foods such as breads or dairy products (more on this in chapter 5) to fall asleep at night. They aren't able to have a full, restful night's sleep, however, because of the remaining effects of caffeine, so they wake up feeling exhausted. Then, because they're so sleepy in the morning, they reach for more caffeine, chocolate, or sugar to get going again. It's very easy to get into this pattern and not know how to break out of it.

For hypersexual chocoholics like Christine, eating chocolate in abundance also plays a role in an imbalanced "sexual metabolism" (what I call the desire for sex, or the sexual appetite). Some people, as described above, clam up, isolate themselves, and feel tense after ingesting a lot of stimulant foods and beverages. Others, like Christine, "act out" or become flamboyant show-offs in response to pep foods. In fact, Christine would become so up, so high, after eating chocolate, that she'd have regular fantasies about becoming a nude dancer or shocking a stranger by flashing her bare breasts at him. In other words, the stimulation Christine received from the chemicals in chocolate made her excited and anxious to receive sexual attention.

What we found in therapy, though, was interesting: Christine's desire for sex and sexual advances was a lot like Cathy's need for compliments and praise. Christine, although she definitely enjoyed physical intercourse, was mainly interested in being validated by it. She felt more worthwhile, more valuable as a woman, if a man was interested in going to bed with her. Getting a man's sexual interest was as much an accomplishment to Christine as an "A" on a test was to Cathy.

The Chocolate Lover's Recovery Program

The Chocoholic's Dream Diet helps stem chocolate cravings using powerful physiological and psychological tools. Because part of why you crave chocolate has to do with *psychology*—your emotions, moods, and personality—The Dream Diet involves self-help psychological exercises. I'm not saying that the cravings are all in your head; they're definitely real. But I am saying that you can use psychological principles, coupled with the specially designed physiological principles of The Dream Diet, to gain control over your cravings.

A big part of learning how to control chocolate cravings and eat chocolate in moderation is recognizing your own patterns and style of chocoholism. If you recognize yourself in this chapter, you've completed a first step. Just by understanding yourself and your motivation, you gain a great deal of control over your compulsions.

Since so much of the Chocolate Lover's desire for chocolate stems from a desire for love and nurturing, my work with these clients involves helping them to feel less deprived of love. This involves assigning them projects designed to help them love themselves more.

If you're a Chocolate Lover, feeling unloved and unnurtured, you'll find that this therapeutic assignment will help by raising your self-esteem and self-love levels:

Beginning today, and continuing every day, I'd like you to do one nice thing for yourself. This could be anything from buying yourself a bouquet of fresh flowers, taking a bubble bath, or taking time out of a busy day to go to the gym. It could mean buying yourself a new outfit. Asking your boss for a raise. Or taking a night-school class just for fun.

By doing something nice just for you, and not for anyone else, you'll start to feel really good about yourself. You'll start to rely on yourself for love, and this in turn will make a dramatic improvement in your relationships with others. Since you won't be expecting or needing others to provide your only source of love, you'll be more free to have fun, loving relationships.

The physical part of gaining control over your chocoholism—The Chocoholic's Dream Diet—appears in the second half of this book. It explains how to keep chocolate—in moderation—in a healthy, low-fat, low-cholesterol diet. This diet, and an understanding of your behavior, are both necessary components in achieving lifelong weight loss.

3

Winter Eating
and Menstrual Blues:
The Situational Chocoholic

For Situational Chocoholics, their on-again, off-again cravings for chocolate can seem maddeningly inconsistent. "Most of the time, I can control my eating," he or she will tell me, "but every now and then, bam! I'll be eating everything chocolate in sight, and still not be able to get enough."

Because of these inconsistent cravings, Situational Chocoholics have more difficulty than other chocoholics. They simply cannot predict how their appetite will react to one bite of chocolate, that is, until they understand their particular "chocoholic cycle."

Some Situational Chocoholics know, for a fact, that their cravings become uncontrollable around their menstrual periods, or around the holidays. And yet, they'll tell me that this knowledge does not stop the cravings.

In this chapter, then, we'll take a look at the whole picture: what your pattern of craving chocolate is, why, and what steps to take.

Monthly Cyclic Chocoholism

Let's start with a little therapeutic assignment: I'd like to ask you to spend the next thirty days charting your chocolate cravings.

Using a large blank sheet of paper, draw five horizontal lines and five vertical lines to make thirty squares. Next, put today's date in the first square and number the remaining squares like a calendar, except you'll be going into next month's dates to fill the thirty squares. This is your "chocoholism calendar," and I'd like you to tape it to your refrigerator door, where it'll be handy and noticeable.

At the end of each day, jot down the following information about your chocolate cravings for the day:

1. Whether you craved chocolate or not.
2. How strong your chocolate cravings were, using a 1 to 10 rating system, with 1 meaning small cravings and 10 meaning unbearable cravings.
3. If it is during your menstrual period, indicate which day you are on within that cycle (e.g., "second day of my period").

If you craved chocolate consistently for four to seven days in a row, but only mildly craved it the rest of the month, then your chocoholism is tied into your monthly hormonal fluctuations. Women aren't the only ones to experience this, because men have definite monthly body temperature and hormonal shifts as well. They just don't end their cycles with an obvious physical event (the menstrual period) like women do. Usually, men who are very aware of their body's signals—for example, those who notice small pains quickly, or feel the effect of eating sugar on their moods right away—are more prone to monthly cyclic chocoholism.

"Monthly Cyclic Chocoholism," as I call it, usually begins within the week before the menstrual period. Some people crave chocolate the whole week; others want it only the day before their period starts. Either way, it's a difficult, sometimes frightening, experience to deal with.

My client Alicia comes to mind. Alicia, a 39-year-old administrator, had one of those faces that reminded you of an actress in a popular television show—she was familiar looking and pleasant to be around. She came to my clinic because she said she was a "Dr. Jekyll and Mr. Hyde"—easygoing and in control most of the time, but right around her period, her mood and her appetite for chocolate would go completely out of control. This had caused Alicia to question her own sanity, and it definitely made her feel out of control with her life, as well as her weight.

"I'll be doing so good with my diet," she told me, "and then it'll get to be *that* time of month. I'll get the taste of a chocolate bar in my mouth, and all I can think about is getting one! It's like I get possessed, and then I *have to* get some chocolate or I go nuts and can't concentrate on anything." Alicia would fight within herself every month, promising herself she wouldn't go near chocolate. Then her cravings would begin. And once again, she'd find herself in the candy section of the grocery store, loading her shopping cart with chocolate bars.

"When I go ahead and eat the chocolate, I really do feel better for a little while. Even the cramps go away for a bit," Alicia explained. "But then I'll get so mad at myself and feel really guilty for going off my diet. And the chocolate cravings always come back again in an hour or so after I've pigged out." It was easy to see why

Alicia was so frustrated when she finally came in to see me.

Alicia used The Chocoholic's Dream Diet to successfully overcome her Monthly Cyclic Chocoholism and regain control of her appetite.

Seasonal Cycles

A number of Situational Chocoholics find themselves in the same situation as my client Pam. She came into my office after reading my book, *The Yo-Yo Syndrome Diet*, because she wanted to stop her weight from fluctuating by 25 pounds every year.

After talking with her, I found that Pam would lose weight every spring and maintain her weight throughout the summer. Then she'd gain it all back again in the winter. "I know exactly what's going on with my weight, but I still can't seem to control myself," Pam complained. "It's like I only care about my weight during the summer because that's when I'll be seen in shorts. In the wintertime, I don't give a damn about what shape I'm in, 'cause I know I can hide in my clothes."

Pam was a "Seasonal Chocoholic," a style of chocoholism which accounts for roughly 25 percent of the chocoholics I've treated and interviewed. Seasonal chocoholics fall into two main categories, which sometimes are difficult to distinguish from one another because of the overlapping symptoms and circumstances:

1. Those whose chocoholism arises from physiological and psychological triggers tied into the winter months.
2. Those whose chocoholism is triggered by the increased availability of chocolate during the holidays.

In the first instance, there are very real physical reasons why chocoholism occurs in some people during the winter months. When the amount of sunshine diminishes, many people experience Seasonal Affective Disorder (SAD). This is literally a withdrawal symptom from lack of full-spectrum lighting as the sun moves farther away from the earth during the winter. Two of the most prominent symptoms of SAD are depression and cravings for carbohydrates, especially chocolate.

SAD appears to be tied into an imbalance and decreased production of a chemical in the brain called serotonin. This chemical influences mood, and when not enough serotonin is created, the result is depression, fatigue, and irritability. The body then signals that it needs help to produce more serotonin, so it produces carbohydrate cravings—breads, sweets, and especially chocolate.

Carbohydrates boost the brain's production of serotonin and also increase the blood sugar level. Both processes make you feel happier and more energetic.

Wintertime weight gain occurs for many very real biological reasons. While a small percentage of SAD sufferers show a reverse tendency—they gain weight and feel depressed in the summer, and then feel better and lose weight in the winter—most SAD sufferers find their appetite normalizes when they're exposed to full-spectrum lighting. For some, this means anxiously awaiting summertime. For extreme SAD sufferers with debilitating symptoms, a medical doctor usually prescribes a home system of special full-spectrum lights. The SAD sufferer spends a prescribed amount of time in front of the lights, and almost always finds the depression lifting and the carbohydrate cravings lessening.

SAD and PMS

Before going on to explain the second type of seasonal chocoholic, I think it's useful to stop and see a very important point. Many monthly cyclic chocoholics experience chocolate cravings because of their Premenstrual Syndrome (PMS)—a combination of debilitating symptoms which appear in conjunction with the hormonal fluctuations of the menstrual period.

SAD and PMS are very similar in their symptoms, and both are largely brought about by a decrease in the brain chemical serotonin. What's interesting to me is that the over-the-counter PMS medications have many of the effects on PMS symptoms as chocolate. So, to me, it seems perfectly understandable why people who suffer from PMS and SAD crave chocolate.

Just consider this: A typical PMS or menstrual cramp over-the-counter medication contains acetaminophen or ibuprofen (painkillers) plus a stimulant (usually caffeine). Chocolate contains many stimulants (particularly theobromine, tyramine, and caffeine), plus it acts as a painkiller in an indirect way by providing pleasure and momentarily blocking conscious awareness of physical and emotional pain.

But wintertime depression isn't all based on physical reasons; there are lots of triggers for wintertime blues that have little to do with the body. Julie, for example, was aware that she'd become depressed starting at Halloween, and would stay feeling down until after New Year's Eve. From October 31 through January 1, Julie would always gain 25 pounds.

"I just get so depressed when the holidays start!" the red-haired registered nurse told me. Julie had struggled with feelings of holiday-related depression since her parents had divorced when she was 32-years-old. "Since Mom and Dad split up, holidays are such a mess. We never know whether to invite Dad or Mom over to the house—you can't have both of them in the same room, or they start to argue and ruin the entire day."

Julie went on to explain that her memories of holidays as a child had been shattered by her parents' divorce. "We used to have these *really special* holidays," she explained tearfully. "I mean, Mom and Dad always put a lot of imagination into hiding our presents on Christmas and leaving us little clues on notepaper about where to find them. And on Halloween and New Year's, we'd always have costume parties at our house. Thanksgiving was special too—we'd go to Grandma Rose's house and she'd have this great dinner with turkey, stuffing, and a thousand different side dishes."

While Julie had always struggled with her weight, she found it increasingly hard to keep from overeating since her parents had abruptly announced their divorce five years earlier ("They never even asked us if we cared before they got a divorce," Julie kept repeating). And since her depression was most pronounced during the holiday season—this is the time of year when Julie most missed being from an intact family—she binged on the most prominent food available: chocolate.

Chocolate's ready availability at holiday time, combined with the increase in depression occurring during the winter, makes seasonal chocoholism almost predictable. I remember, years ago, when I gave a large Halloween party. I bought hundreds of miniature chocolate candies and arranged them on crystal dishes on a huge buffet table.

Since I was on an unrealistically stringent diet at the time, I swore I wouldn't eat one bite of the chocolate. And, oh, how deprived I felt when I smelled those chocolate bars I was decoratively arranging. I remember that the Butterfinger bars especially tempted me, with their smell of sweet peanut butter and chocolate. But still, I resisted because my diet forbade any chocolate.

Well, I did okay the night of the party—I didn't eat any chocolate at all. But the next day, I felt tense, irritable, and uneasy, because deep down, I was feeling deprived. After all, I had spent all evening the night before watching other people devour my favorite food and I wasn't "allowed" to eat any myself. In other words, I had felt jealous and full of self-pity because "poor me" wasn't allowed to eat any candy.

Can you guess what I did next? After a whole day of feeling deprived and resentful, I went straight to the grocery store that evening of November 1, 1984, and bought the following items: an extra-large Hershey's chocolate bar, an extra-large Butterfinger bar, and a small carton of double-chocolate Haagen-Dazs ice cream. Then I went home and ate the whole thing.

I felt ill, but no longer deprived. Instead, I felt contempt for myself, weak willed because I had broken my precious diet. I was a failure, I thought, for succumbing to my chocolate cravings. In fact, I felt so bad about myself that evening that I finally "hit bottom" with my chocolate addiction.

That's why I decided to do something about my chocoholism so that I wouldn't feel deprived, and also so that I wouldn't go on any more chocolate-eating binges. And that's when I started to develop The Chocoholic's Dream Diet.

As a result, I'm happy to report, November 1, 1984, was the last time I ate chocolate out of control. Since that time, using the principles you'll learn in this book, I've dropped 55 pounds and maintained a steady weight

of 130 to 132 pounds (I'm five feet nine inches tall).
And I've learned how to eat chocolate in a sane manner.

As a Situational Chocoholic, I used to binge around
the holidays because so much chocolate was around.
We'd always have two boxes of See's candies under the
Christmas tree, and it was considered antisocial to say
no to chocolate when it was passed around.

One of my patients, Diane, also binged on chocolate around Christmas, but for different reasons. Diane, a
43-year-old elementary school teacher, was rather slender but still worried about her weight. At five feet five
inches, she fit comfortably into size 10 off the rack, but
believing she was fat, Diane chronically dieted.

Her dieting efforts became especially concerted in
the months before Christmas. Diane explained: "I always go on a super low-cal diet around November first.
That way, I can be skinny for my family Christmas
reunion, and I can eat as much as I want at Christmas
dinner."

Diane's Christmastime starve-binge routine never
worked out like she planned, though. Yes, she would
lose enough weight to fit into a size 8 dress for Christmas. But then, when she'd start on her "planned binge,"
her plans would go awry because she always spent the
most time eating the chocolate treats—candies, cookies, pudding, and cake—and she'd keep eating chocolate until way past New Year's Day. "I always lose 15
pounds before Christmas," Diane said solemnly. "But
then I end up gaining it back, plus more weight, right
after Christmas."

The Chocoholic's Dream Diet works for all three
types of Situational Chocoholics—the Monthly Cyclic
Chocoholic and the two types of Seasonal Chocoholic—
for three main reasons:

—The foods in the diet, while healthy and easy to find, are specially chosen to provide amino acid and mineral combinations to help the brain chemical serotonin remain at normal levels. This helps to reduce chocolate and carbohydrate cravings as well as to alleviate depressive mood swings.

—The daily chocolate snack helps because you won't feel deprived from your favorite food. That way, you won't be so tempted to go on a chocolate-eating binge right before your menstrual period or during the holidays.

—You'll feel mentally and physically fit using The Dream Diet. And because you'll already feel so good, so "charged" and alive, you won't need to lean on chocolate to make you feel good.

"I Can't Stop Eating!"
The Chocolate Binger's Panic

I was giving a talk late one Tuesday night in a downtown Los Angeles auditorium, and I was talking about the addiction to food. Making an analogy with the alcoholic who, after drinking one beer, can't stop drinking, I was talking about people who lose control of their appetites after eating one bite of a certain type of food.

"Chocolate," a woman muttered matter-of-factly from the audience. "Chocolate."

I knew why she was saying that without asking her, but I wanted the rest of the audience to hear, firsthand, the experience of someone who ate chocolate addictively. Chocolate bingers always recognize themselves as being out of control with their chocoholism, but for people who are able to eat one M & M and then leave the package alone, binge eating seems like one giant excuse for a lack of willpower.

"Chocolate triggers binges in you?" I asked the woman, inviting her to expand on her "chocolate" declaration.

"It's true," said the kindly looking lady. She glanced at the students sitting beside her before continuing, as if to see their reaction to her admission of being out of control with chocolate. Many of the students were nodding their heads knowingly, while others were sitting with arms folded across their chests and wearing puzzled expressions.

The lady said, "Every time I eat chocolate, I can't stop eating! I've tried everything to control myself, like just buying one candy bar at a time so I can't pig out on a whole box of candy." The woman looked down, visibly upset. "But it never fails: Once I get hold of a candy bar, I always end up driving back to a store and buying more. It's like I have to have a 'fix' or something, like I can't control myself until I eat something chocolaty."

At this point, several of the other students chimed in that they, too, felt out of control after one bite of chocolate. And I knew just what they meant, because I'm a Chocolate Binger myself.

This Doesn't Mean I Have to Give Up Chocolate. Does It?

Chocolate Bingers often attempt to "cure" their chocoholism by completely abstaining from chocolate. But this usually results in the chocoholic feeling deprived, followed by an enormous, months-long chocolate-eating binge.

Do Chocolate Bingers have to give up chocolate in order to stay in control of their appetites? The answer, which you'll learn in this chapter as well as the remainder of this book, is, "Almost never." That is, almost every chocoholic can learn to eat chocolate *in certain forms that are different for everyone* and still have an appetite that's under control.

The appetite really is, after all, the key element in weight control. If you weren't hungry all the time, if you didn't crave chocolate or other foods, you'd have no problem keeping slim, right? If your appetite were under control, you wouldn't feel deprived, as if you were starving on a diet, correct? This is why it's so important to understand the concept of binge foods: Only after you eliminate your binge food from your diet will your appetite for that food, and usually other foods, disappear or decrease. In other words, the binge food is triggering your appetite and making you want to eat uncontrollably.

The Main Binge Trigger

I have found over and over in treating and talking with Chocolate Bingers that the main culprit in binge eating is refined sugar. In other words, you lose control of your appetite because of the refined sugar in the chocolate candy, ice cream, frozen yogurt, pie, cake, pudding, or cookies—not because of the chocolate.

Let's take a look at why I firmly believe this is so: Refined sugar instantly raises the blood sugar level of the body. This makes the Chocolate Binger feel anxious, tense, and a bit excited. That anxiety and tension, in turn, can feel exactly like physical hunger; the two feelings are often confused as being one and the same. One minute you're fine, and the next minute you're starving. That *sudden* hunger really means that you're feeling anxious and you don't know how else to deal with it other than by eating. So instead of your brain registering, "anxiety," it says to you, "I'm starving."

Binge eating, then, becomes a form of coping with nervous anxiety. Of course, overeating only makes you more anxious because of the guilt and self-anger you feel when you binge. And there's more:

Chocolate, combined with refined sugar, can make you particularly tense because of chemicals contained in chocolate called "theobromine" and "tyramine." These stimulants, combined with the caffeine in chocolate, instantly raise the blood pressure and make you feel aroused but jittery. By the way, this blood pressure raising effect is the main reason why you should never feed chocolate to your pets: It can actually be lethal because their little blood vessels can't take the change in blood pressure.

In humans, though, all this stimulation from refined sugar, combined with theobromine, tyramine, and caffeine, does result in a "high" feeling after eating sugared chocolate (that is, chocolate sweetened with refined white cane sugar). However, a short time after eating refined sugar, the blood sugar level drops from above normal to below normal. In other words, you "crash" from the high you were on.

What happens next is exactly like the behavior seen in cocaine or speed addicts: The "crash" makes you feel lethargic, so you reach for more of your stimulant agent (in this case, chocolate) to boost your energy and spirits again. Since sugared chocolate is causing *and* undoing the "crash," it's easy to get into a vicious cycle of dependency on chocolate. In other words, a chocolate binge.

Sugar Addiction and Alcoholism

Perhaps the most striking observation I've made in working with chocoholics is the high incidence (over 95 percent) of alcoholism in the parents and grandparents of chocoholics. Almost all chocoholics have either parents or grandparents who drank alcohol in a dependent or abusive manner. Even my clients who initially denied that alcoholism runs in their family usually find, after asking other family members, that Grandpa was, in fact, an alcoholic, but nobody in the family ever talked about it. Instead, they'd say that Grandpa died of cirrhosis of the liver, a heart attack, or some other alcoholism-related disease.

This discussion is not intended to point a finger of fault, such as "your grandad's to blame for your chocoholism." But if you're a Chocolate Binger, it's important to understand the role of alcoholism in your chocolate addiction.

The bulk of studies on alcoholism in families overwhelmingly point to a genetic link that causes an alcoholic predisposition—that is, *the possibility is there to a greater degree than in people from nonalcoholic families*. While about 10 percent of people in the general population become alcoholic, having one alcoholic parent increases your chances of being alcoholic to over 30 percent. And if your mother and your father were both alcoholic, your risk of being alcoholic is greater than 50 percent.

What this means to the Chocolate Binger is this: Alcohol and sugar are almost identical in their molecular structure. The result is that people prone to alcoholism have a reaction to sugar identical to an alcoholic reaction to alcohol. This is a combination of changes in the brain's chemistry and electrical activity and a subjective feeling of anxiously wanting more alcohol or sugar.

The alcoholic body has a difficult time distinguishing between alcohol and sugar and wants to binge on either substance. And this especially makes sense when you consider that alcohol is made of food—wine is fermented fruit, beer is breads, vodka is potatoes, etc.

I've also found that female children and grandchildren of alcoholics are more apt to pick refined sugar over alcohol as their "feel-good drug" of choice. I believe this occurs for two reasons:

1. Social pressures train young females to be nice, good little girls. These pressures cause females to pick, what I call, "the good girl's drug": sugar.
2. Most likely, the girl's mother was a compulsive eater and sugar binger herself. The little girl watched her mother overeat sugar and use sugar as a stress-management tool, and this reinforced the girl's likelihood of abusing sugar later on in life.

The pairing of compulsive overeaters/sugar bingers with alcoholics is a classic family scenario seen by psychotherapists, such as myself, who specialize in treating addictions. In fact, in the Schuman study mentioned in chapter 2, an interesting tidbit of information came out: Alcoholics rarely crave chocolate. Their particular binge food is usually extremely spicy, salty foods. This makes sense to me, because people who crave spicy food usually need more intensity in their lives than other people. And if you're numbed by the effects of alcohol, delicate flavors can be difficult to detect. I also suppose that chocolate and beer would make a pretty awful combination.

I think you'll agree, though, that it's no wonder why people binge on chocolate. And we haven't even talked yet about the role of how delicious chocolate is! It's so interesting to me to look at the combination of effects from refined sugar, the stimulants in chocolate, and the role of alcoholism in the family. Combined, they can make a Chocolate Binger feel weak, helpless over his or her appetite, and completely devoid of willpower. As you can see, though, the problem is that the sugared chocolate has power over the Chocolate Binger and he or she is at its mercy.

Just as the alcoholic cannot stop with one beer, so too is the Chocolate Binger out of control after eating one bite of sugared chocolate.

The Chocolate Binger's Treatment Approach

If you are a true Chocolate Binger, you know that you can't have one piece of sugared chocolate without feeling the need to eat a whole candy store full of chocolate. On the other hand, you are *not* a true Chocolate Binger if you only *occasionally* binge (or want to binge) after eating a piece of sugared chocolate. You, instead, would fit into one of the other styles of chocoholism.

All the styles of chocoholism will be following the same Dream Diet; however, the Chocolate Binger will be making one notable exception: He or she must not eat any chocolate sweetened with refined sugar!

The Chocoholic's Dream Diet is filled, you'll see in the pages to come, with lots and lots of alternatives to sugared chocolate. In fact, by using the recipes in chapter 10, you'll find that you won't even miss refined sugar in your chocolate treats. As I've said before, too, it's important that you not feel deprived if your diet is to be successful over a lifetime. So, rest assured that chocolate will still be a part of your life.

The difference is that it will be refined sugar-free chocolate. By eating chocolate without sugar, you'll find your appetite will stay in control and you won't *want* to overeat chocolate. Instead, you'll be satisfied with a small portion.

I've heard the following statement so many times that I feel I'd better include it right here. People will say, "But I've tried eating sugar-free chocolate and I still binge!" Then I ask them what sugar-free chocolate they're talking about, and almost always they tell me it's chocolate frozen yogurt or a sugar-free-chocolate ice-cream confection (like a fudge pop or a chocolate-covered vanilla ice-cream bar).

What I tell them is important for you to understand: sugar free doesn't always mean sugar free. In the case of frozen yogurt, I've found that people binge on frozen yogurt sweetened with refined sugar. Many people mistakenly assume that just because frozen yogurt is billed as a low-fat, low-calorie health food, it couldn't possibly have refined sugar in it. But the truth is that unless the yogurt shop specifically advertises sugar-free yogurt, it probably is sweetened with refined sugar. It's very important that you ask to see an ingredients list whenever you order chocolate frozen yogurt. It's also important that you not eat sugared carob toppings on your yogurt, because, again, it's a fallacy to assume that just because carob is seen as a health food, it contains no sugar. Most carob candies are loaded with refined sugar!

If you've binged on sugar-free-chocolate frozen confections, you've probably also unknowingly been eating a sweetening agent that acts in the same way as sugar: corn syrup. Many products labeled "sugar free" actually contain high amounts of corn syrup, which is another form of sugar that commonly triggers binges. If you are a true Chocolate Binger, then avoid corn syrup and sugar syrup just as you would avoid refined sugar.

As you'll see further in chapter 5, The Chocoholic's Dream Diet is based on a special selection of healthy, tasty foods designed to reduce your chocolate cravings. You'll learn, as you continue to read, why fructose, honey, and NutraSweet may be the best alternative sweeteners for your chocolate treats. And when you eat the foods in The Dream Diet, combined with your daily sugar-free chocolate snack, you'll find that your chocolate binging disappears.

Most people report that their out-of-control cravings are eliminated after a month on The Dream Diet. A small percentage of people say they still miss eating a large amount of chocolate, but that at least their appetite is under control and manageable.

Additional Tips for Chocolate Bingers

Avoiding sugared chocolate is easier said (or read) than done. As a recovering (since 1984) Chocolate Binger, let me share with you some of the survival methods I used until my cravings for sugared chocolate subsided:

• *I had to stay completely out of chocolate candy aisles at the grocery and department stores.* Just the sight and smell of sugared chocolate would shake up my motivation and make me want to go on a binge.

• *I had to avoid handling sugared chocolate treats.* I found that the mere act of scooping chocolate ice cream for my sons drove me crazy with desire to binge. The texture of the ice cream against the ice-cream scoop, combined with the sight of the ice cream, made it difficult for me to stay on my Dream Diet. I had to tell my boys to serve their own ice cream; if they had been too young to do that, I would have limited their ice cream to an occasional treat at school (so I wouldn't be tempted), or I would have asked my husband to scoop it for them.

I still don't handle ice cream or other chocolate treats, out of respect for the permanence of chocoholism. In other words, Chocolate Binging is not something you outgrow with time. Just as an alcoholic is always an alcoholic no matter how many years he or she stays sober, so a Chocolate Binger is always a Chocolate Binger—no matter how thin he or she gets.

• *I couldn't have any sugared chocolate in the house.* Before I went on The Dream Diet, my husband usually kept a box of thin chocolate candies in our freezer. And during my binges, I would always eat them as quickly as he could replace them.

I thought I could control myself around the candy after going on The Dream Diet, but I found that the sight of those chocolates made me *very* uncomfortable whenever I'd open up the freezer. I remember clearly the night about three weeks after I began my Dream Diet. I was about to go on an eating binge with those frozen chocolates. I panicked, thinking, *What should I do?* I really, really wanted to eat them! They looked so good, and I thought to myself, *I'll eat just one and then I'll stop.*

Thank goodness I was able to stop in my tracks and be honest with myself. I knew I was just rationalizing to say I'd have just one chocolate. So before I could risk the possibility of blowing my Dream Diet, I threw all the candies down the garbage disposal, paper wrappings and all.

I'd highly recommend that you get rid of all the sugared chocolate in your house, car, purse, or desk drawer right now. Please don't rationalize, as I did, by saying something like, "I hate to waste the money I spent on this chocolate. I'll give it to my neighbor." Most people will eat the chocolate before they have a chance to give it to their neighbor! Don't take any chances by having sugared chocolate around.

• *I had to admit whom I was buying chocolate treats for.* Another vivid memory of my early Dream Diet days was the time I was shopping with my husband and I *insisted* that he buy a beautifully wrapped box of chocolate candies. "This is a special treat for you, honey," I told him. "You deserve it."

He looked at me as if I were half out of my mind, but then reluctantly agreed to keep it in our shopping cart. As if that weren't bad enough, as soon as we got in our car, I *insisted* that he unwrap the box of chocolates and eat one. "Come on," I urged until he finally complied. I enjoyed unwrapping that box of chocolate for him as much as if I were a kid opening a Christmas present!

I then watched, totally absorbed, as he popped a chocolate into his mouth. "How does it taste? How does it taste?" I insisted on knowing immediately.

Then I caught myself, suddenly realizing what I was doing—I was trying to go on an eating binge vicariously. That is, I was trying to derive pleasure from my husband's blow-by-blow description of his chocolate-eating experience. And if I hadn't seen this in myself, if I hadn't looked at my motivations honestly, I definitely would have ended up eating that whole box of chocolates myself. Because in the end, I had to admit, I had bought that chocolate box for me and not for my husband.

• *I had to stop making chocolate candy as Christmas gifts.* It was a family tradition that I had continued into adulthood: Every Christmas, my mother and I would make chocolate-covered toffee candy. We'd make huge batches, put them in decorative containers, and then give them as gifts to coworkers, neighbors, and casual acquaintances. Everyone always loved the candy and put in their "order" to be on the candy gift list the following holiday season.

The first Christmas of my Dream Diet, I had already convinced myself that making candy would be a foolish mistake. Instead, I gave small gifts of cologne. So, I didn't get into any problems myself, but my patient Lynette sure did.

It was November 1987 and we'd been discussing "holiday survival plans" in our group-therapy sessions since October. Still, Lynette insisted that she couldn't give up baking chocolate chip cookies as Christmas gifts. The group implored her to reconsider, but she was firmly resistant.

I don't think I need to go into too much detail about what happened because you can probably guess. I received a phone call from Lynette around three P.M. the week before Christmas. "Doreen!" she cried frantically. "You and the group members were right!"

Lynette went on to explain how she had been making chocolate chip cookies and chocolate cupcakes for Christmas gifts, when she had decided to taste the first batch, "just to make sure everything tasted good." What happened next was a one-hour eating binge, with Lynette anxiously eating the entire batch, plus much of the uncooked cookie dough. By the time she called me, she felt sick and disgusted with herself.

After talking, we decided the best course of action was for Lynette's teenage daughter to complete the baking process. I then asked Lynette to leave her house until all the cookies and cupcakes had been prepared and packaged in gift boxes. That was the last year Lynette prepared dessert as Christmas gifts.

• *I made it a point to have a sugar-free chocolate treat every day.* This is an important part of The Dream Diet: To avoid feeling deprived (which would lead to an eating binge), you need to have one daily sugar-free chocolate treat as described in Part II of this book.

I know for a fact I couldn't have gotten my 55 pounds off and kept it off without my daily chocolate treat.

• *I had to learn how to deal with the chocolates my coworkers brought into work.* There were always boxes of chocolate-covered doughnuts at the alcoholism treatment hospital where I worked when I began my Dream Diet. I always felt this was beyond my control: After all, I hadn't bought the doughnuts, so who was I to complain about their presence?

And yet the sight of those doughnuts really bothered me, and made me want to overeat. I found that I could take the box and put it up on a shelf where I couldn't look *into* it and see the doughnuts, yet the box was still visible to anyone who wanted a doughnut.

When people at work would bring in homemade sugared chocolate treats and insist that I try one, I had to think fast. Explaining my diet to them usually resulted in a philosophical debate about the "correct" way to diet, with them saying that one little cookie wouldn't hurt my diet. True, one sugared cookie isn't fattening in itself. But when you're a sugar binger, there's no such thing as one bite of something containing sugar.

I now confidently tell "sugar pushers" that I cannot eat their sugary fare because of allergies I have. This is true in the sense of an alcoholic being allergic to alcohol and a sugar binger being allergic to sugar. I don't break out in hives, but I do have very, very uncomfortable symptoms (tension, anxiety, and a desire to binge), which I choose to avoid at all costs.

And with The Chocoholic's Dream Diet, I don't miss sugared chocolate at all!

• *I had to learn to read labels on all foods I was buying to avoid hidden sources of sugar and corn syrup.* As mentioned before, sugar free doesn't always mean sugar free. And many of the "light" products, such as "light" chocolate ice cream, are loaded with sugar.

Make it a firm rule with yourself: Always read the ingredients list before you buy anything. If it has sugar or corn syrup in it, or if there are no ingredients listed, put it back.

5

The Hershey's High:
The Euphoric Chocoholic

The Euphoric Chocoholic almost always insists that he or she eats chocolate because it tastes so good. And, of course, chocolate is the most delicious flavor in the world. A true chocoholic would never think about ordering vanilla when chocolate is an option. As a matter of fact, I've walked out of frozen-yogurt shops that weren't offering chocolate as a featured flavor.

But the flavor of chocolate isn't always the most seductive temptation for the Euphoric Chocoholic. Instead, if Euphorics *really* think about chocolate's appeal, they'll usually admit that eating chocolate makes them *feel* really good.

Euphoric Chocoholics are emotional, sensitive people who are especially sensitive to the way chemicals and drugs affect their body and emotions. Most Euphorics are very aware that eating certain foods has a profound effect on their state of mind and body.

Let me explain: Most foods contain powerful mood-altering, psychoactive chemicals that can alter the moods we're feeling. Sugar, as described in chapter 4, plays havoc on the body's energy cycles. And Euphoric Chocoholics are more aware of this effect than most— they also tend to use, even at times abuse, food's mood-altering effects.

Euphoric Chocoholics are more likely than others to use stimulant foods such as caffeine, colas, chocolate, and artificial sweeteners to increase their energy levels. Sharon, a 37-year-old divorced mother of two, exemplified this Euphoric tendency to use foods as drugs.

As manager of the city's busiest bookstore in a bustling mall, Sharon found there were never enough hours in the day to get everything down. Every weekday morning, the alarm would ring at 5:30, and Sharon would reluctantly wake up feeling exhausted and dreading the day ahead of her. She'd put on a strong pot of chocolate-flavored gourmet coffee and would start getting the kids up and dressed for school.

In the meantime, Sharon would rush to get dressed herself. Never feeling like she had time for breakfast, she'd instead down three or four cups of coffee before heading out the door to face the morning traffic. Inside, Sharon's heart would usually be racing as she urgently fought to get the kids and herself downtown on time.

After opening the bookstore and making sure the cash registers were ready to go, Sharon would head to her cramped office in the back of the store. Then, she'd take a deep breath and pull open her desk drawer where she stashed her supply of candy bars. Snickers and M & M's were her favorite, but at times like these, Sharon would settle for anything sweet and chocolaty. She needed the boost from chocolate's ingredients— sugar, theobromine, tyramine, and caffeine—to keep her going throughout her hectic day. So much work, so many problems, too much unwanted responsibility.

All day long, until it was time to pick up the kids and go home, Sharon would rely on coffee and chocolate bars to pep her up. At night, she'd be drained and dead tired. Still, her system would stay revved up from all the stimulants she'd ingested during the day. Sharon would lie awake in bed, her heart pounding rapidly. Her mind said sleep, but her body said no. She'd toss and turn, fighting within herself, until at last sometime long after midnight she'd fall asleep.

The next day, Sharon would be so tired that she had no choice, she felt, but to turn toward the chocolate and coffee again.

Sharon's story is typical of the overstressed person who turns to food to regulate his or her moods and energy levels. But there's more than one style of using food in a self-medicating manner. In fact, there are as many styles of Euphoric Chocoholism as there are emotions, moods, and energy levels.

Understanding Your Food-Mood Style

If you eat one piece or serving of something—a candy bar, slice of cake, hamburger, or whatever—it doesn't necessarily mean you are trying to regulate your mood and energy level. But if you feel anxiously compelled to eat a lot of a certain type of food *all of a sudden*, you are most likely eating food in a Euphoric manner. That is, you feel a distressing emotion such as stress, depression, anxiety, or boredom (which is really loneliness combined with frustration that life is too routine) and you want to feel better.

The chemicals, ingredients, textures, tastes, and smells in most foods have definite effects on emotions and energy levels. After studying the individual effects of each mood/energy-regulating characteristic of foods, I've found a very consistent correlation between food cravings and emotional states.

Here's an example of how this correlation works in

a cycle: Betty feels depressed, so she reaches for a food which she knows intuitively from past experience will ease her depression. She chooses chocolate ice cream. It makes her feel better because of the natural antidepressant ingredients, textures, and smells in chocolate ice cream. However, she eats so much of it that she feels even more depressed later. This depression, about her weight and feeling out of control, leads Betty to eat more chocolate ice cream the next day. And the cycle can go on for a lifetime.

Without going into a chemistry lecture, let me briefly explain how a food like chocolate ice cream is an antidepressant. When you look at the combination of effects from the ingredients in chocolate ice cream, you see that they trigger a reaction in people much the way prescription antidepressant drugs do.

Take a look at a breakdown of some of the properties in chocolate ice cream:

Ingredient/Characteristic	Effect on Mood/Energy
Choline	Soothing
L-Tryptophane with carbohydrates	Calming
Creamy Texture	Comforting
Sugar	Temporarily Energizing
PEA	Feeling Loved
Theobromine	Temporarily Energizing
Tyramine	Temporarily Energizing
Caffeine	Temporarily Energizing
Magnesium	Relaxing
Pyrazine	Pleasure inducing

And this is an incomplete list! This list, however, should show you that chocolate ice cream makes you feel soothed and comforted while at the same time reenergizing you (if only temporarily). In other words, after eating chocolate ice cream, you feel renewed and ready to go! This is extremely similar to the way that prescription antidepressant drugs affect the mind and body. To me, chocolate ice cream is an incredibly powerful antidepressant drug, and it's over-the-counter!

All the other foods that people commonly overeat have similar food-mood correlations. I've found in treating clients and in talking to people all across the country that, consistently, the connections between mood and emotion appearing on the chart below always occur.

I've had people from all walks of life ask me what their food cravings say about their personality. I always give them an answer based on the material I've compiled in the following chart. And always people say, "You're absolutely right! That's exactly how I am."

I've chosen to present to you a list of commonly overeaten foods, together with the emotions that usually lead to cravings for that food. Instead of going into detail about how I've come up with this information, let me just tell you that each food on the list below contains chemicals, textures, and smells that break down just like the example on chocolate ice cream.

The only exception to the outline on this chart seems to occur when an extremely positive or negative emotion has been paired with a certain food. For example, if Mom always served you chicken soup when you were sick, you may feel nauseated every time you smell chicken broth—regardless of the chemical properties in the soup. Or, if Mom always fixed you a special snack of cookies and milk after school, you may have paired that snack with feeling loved. And that would have nothing to do with chemistry at all, would it?

In general, though, I've found my research results on food and mood, as outlined below, to be incredibly accurate. For Euphoric Chocoholics, this chart can be useful in not only looking at why a particular type of chocolate is craved, but also why you, or someone you know, overeats other types of food.

Food	Associated Emotional and Personality Traits
Chocolate candy bars, plain	You desire stimulation, or feel deprived of love.
Crunchy chocolate candy, including chocolate bars with nuts	You feel frustrated, anxious, or angry because of stress or lack of love.
Chocolate ice cream	You feel depressed, usually because of stress or difficulty in a relationship.
Chocolate chip, rocky road, or any crunchy chocolate ice cream	You are holding anger in, or feel angry at yourself, resulting in depression.
Mint chocolate chip ice cream	You feel lethargic and frustrated because you've got more responsibilities than time or motivation.
Chocolate pudding	You desire comfort, nurturing, and hugs.

Chocolate cake	You feel empty, insecure, possibly from lack of love.
Hot chocolate	You have saved up hurt feelings throughout the day, and now desire to ease your ego so you can sleep.
Crunchy, high-fat foods (fried chicken; chips; etc.)	You feel empty because of frustration or anger.
Spicy or salty foods	You are a risk taker, either physically or emotionally.
Crunchy spicy foods (spicy chips or nuts; thin-crusted pizza)	You feel frustrated or angry because life seems dull.
Spicy foods topped with dairy products (pizza with extra cheese; food with cheese and sour cream)	You feel depressed because life seems dull.
Dairy products	You feel depressed or unloved; desire nurturing and comfort.
Baked goods	You feel tense, desire to relax. May also feel life is empty.

Crunchy foods topped with dairy products (crackers and cheese); crispy crust pizza; crisp salad topped with blue cheese dressing; ice cream with chips, nuts, or crisp chocolate coating)	You hold anger, resentment, and/or frustration in, resulting in depression.
Sugary sweets	You desire to feel energetic or to overcome burnout.
Colas, diet or regular	You feel overwhelmed by work or chores; desire to have more energy; also desire to have more sexual energy.
Hamburgers and other high-fat fast foods	You feel empty or dissatisfied with some aspects of life. May also feel insecure or inadequate in some area of life.

In chapter 7, we'll be taking a closer look at ways to eliminate chocolate and other food cravings by making sure your mineral levels are balanced and healthy. The Chocoholic's Dream Diet takes into account that all chocoholics crave their favorite foods for very real reasons.

You'll find, as my patients and I have, that after a month on The Dream Diet, you'll weigh less and feel better and more alert. Your chocolate cravings will also be lessened to the point where you'll be very satisfied with the chocolate snack provided on The Dream Diet.

And by understanding the food-mood connections, you'll be in a better position to stop yourself from compulsively binge eating. The best method to use is one that sounds suspiciously simple, but one that people constantly tell me really works and is very powerful:

The next time you feel very hungry suddenly— meaning, out of the blue—promise me you won't go near any food for fifteen minutes. Get out of the house if you have to, or throw the tempting food down the garbage disposal (not the trash, because sometimes desperate people dig it back out again). No matter what you have to do, don't eat anything for fifteen minutes after first feeling hunger pangs.

Then, ask yourself: "Could I possibly be *feeling* an emotion I'm uncomfortable with? Am I feeling drained and wanting to use food as a pick-me-up?" Most people find that by using this two-step method, they're able to get their food cravings to a manageable proportion, so that they feel in control of their appetite and actions.

If after these steps you still feel hungry for chocolate, then choose one of the snacks outlined in chapters 10 and 11.

6

Eating in Secret:
The Closet Chocoholic

Every evening after dinner, Brenda patiently waited until her family went to bed. She'd always give an excuse why she wanted to stay up. "I want to finish this chapter in the book I'm reading," she'd tell her husband. Or, "Johnny Carson's having that comedian I like so much on tonight."

She wouldn't dare to admit her true motivations for staying awake while the others slept—to be alone with her favorite chocolate cake and ice cream. About a half hour after her husband had gone to bed, after Brenda was sure she couldn't hear him rustling in the bedroom anymore, she'd make her move.

Quietly, so softly that no one could possibly hear her, Brenda would walk into the kitchen. And then, as slowly as she could so that no noise was audible, Brenda would open the freezer door and lift out the carton of ice cream. She'd hold her breath while lifting the carton's lid, so that the sound of the air suction and cardboard rubbing against one another wouldn't awaken anyone.

Sometimes, Brenda would think she heard someone coming, so she'd quickly but quietly shove the ice cream away in a cupboard. But when she was alone, and when she finally had successfully retrieved her chocolate ice cream and cake without a sound, Brenda would stand in the laundry room where no one could see her.

Being alone with her chocolate was utter bliss and luxury to Brenda. Alone, with no one trying to take the chocolate away from her. Alone, where no one could criticize her for going off her diet. Alone, so that she didn't even have to think about what she was doing.

In truth, though, Brenda isn't alone in her behavior. There are thousands, perhaps millions, of Closet Chocoholics—people who feel the need to sneak and hide when they eat their favorite food. Some hide candy bars in the bottom of their purse; some keep chocolate cupcakes hidden in the glove compartment; some stoop down behind open refrigerator doors so that others won't see them eating chocolate with utter abandonment. And I've had clients tell me that they kept chocolate hidden in the bathroom, where they could eat in complete privacy.

But the person the Closet Chocoholic most wants to hide from is himself or herself.

Sneak-Eating and Self-Esteem

I've talked to and treated hundreds of Closet Chocoholics who were single people living alone. And yet, even though they were in the sad predicament of not really having someone who cared in their lives, they still felt afraid that someone else might "catch" them eating something fattening.

My client Sue comes to mind when I think of someone who would sneak-eat, even though there was no one in her life to hide the eating from. During her first therapy session, Sue blurted out that the only way she was going to be able to recover from compulsively eating chocolate was to remove her large stash of candy bars from her car. I walked out to the parking lot to help her, and together we filled up my medium-sized office trash can with boxes of Hershey's bars, Nestlé Crunch bars, and dozens of crumpled old candy wrappers.

With Closet Chocoholics like Sue, the compulsivity of eating chocolate isn't just the appeal of the candy. Instead, the rush of sneaking—the aura of "badness" and "naughtiness"—is a big part of the appeal. Most people have enjoyed the thrill of being naughty, in a harmless sort of way. Feeling the dangerous excitement of possibly being caught, the Closet Chocoholic who completes an uninterrupted eating binge may congratulate herself for getting away with an ingeniously masterminded plan.

Closet Chocoholism is also a silent form of rebellion against real or perceived pressures to be a "good girl," pressures which usually start in childhood. Sue learned early in life that she received tons of attention and praise for being sweet and getting "A's" on her report card. Her parents constantly referred to her as "our problem-free child." So how could Sue let her parents down? She found that complying to others' wishes was the fastest route to gaining approval—a habit which followed her into adulthood.

It's normal for overly compliant people, though, to rebel from time to time, because no one can maintain a false persona of being in a cheerful, understanding mood all the time. In my practice, I've found that many "good girls" silently try to regain control over their lives by gorging on food when others aren't looking.

Many times, these "good girls" grew up in households where a lot of attention was paid to their weight and figures. Messages such as, "Better cut down on the calories because your rear end is starting to get big," are common in Closet Chocoholic households. In other words, part of being a "good girl" implicitly means watching out for fattening foods and calories. Sadly, the young Closet Chocoholic is usually unaware of the fact that it is her body, and therefore her right to regulate what foods she eats and what figure she chooses to maintain.

Sneak-eating usually starts in childhood. This is not a simple case of children stealing cookies from the cookie jar, although that *can* be one symptom of early childhood Closet Chocoholism. Instead, sneak-eating is a process where the person feels unsafe in indulging in pleasurable obsessive eating around others. There's a deep underlying fear that if she is caught eating something "bad" (ice cream, cake, candy, etc.), that the "privilege" of eating this food will be suspended. And, on top of that, she'll be punished by having the other person see her as less than perfect.

To the Closet Chocoholic, it's easier to hide her imperfect behavior—such as obsessive eating of chocolate —from the rest of the world, and to present the face of a competent superwoman or supergirl for everyone else to see. But she also denies to herself that she's sneak-eating. In other words, she's not only hiding from others but from herself, too.

What's particularly interesting to me is that sneak-eaters are very often extremely accomplished women. Every aspect of their life—career, academics, possessions, and family—appears to be under control. But, for the sneak-eater, a very important part of her life—eating and weight—is completely out of control.

Breaking the Eat-and-Sneak Cycle

Closet Chocoholics who examine their motivations for sneak-eating are far less apt to continue closet overeating than people who never take a look at their reasons for sneak-eating. My client Linda, for example, said that I was the first person she'd ever admitted her sneak-eating habits to. Just by talking about her secretive eating, Linda found she wasn't comfortable the next time she began to sneak-eat. After being honest with me about her sneak-eating, it was difficult to hide *what she was really doing* from herself.

I believe that self-honesty is a real key factor in breaking any addictive cycle. This is because so much of compulsive eating, drinking, shopping, etc., is really a way of avoiding looking inside oneself. In other words, many people engage in addictions because they're running away from something inside themselves, or something in their life, that they don't want to examine.

I've had many Closet Chocoholic clients who were indulging in chocolate binges to avoid looking at their unhappy marriages or jobs. Other clients were afraid to look at how much anger they were carrying around inside themselves. And still others were struggling with insecurities—"Am I an okay person?"—and thought, mistakenly, that if they admitted this fear to themselves, then somehow it would be true that they were inadequate.

I, and the chocoholics I have treated, had to stop running from fears in order to comfortably let go of the addiction. There are many ways to do this: support groups such as Overeaters Anonymous, therapy with an eating disorder specialist, talking with a trusted friend, or even writing down everything that comes to mind on a private pad of paper.

Here are some steps Closet Chocoholics can take, in addition to introspection, when the urge to sneak-eat begins:

1. Remember that no matter whom you hide from, or how much you deny to yourself what you're doing, the calories from your binge will show up on *your* body. In the end, it probably doesn't matter to anyone else, as much as it does to you, how much you weigh or how you feel inside your body.

2. Also consider this: Sneak-eating really isn't as much fun as you may believe. If you're really honest with yourself, I think you'll agree that sneak-eating feels crummy and makes you feel bad about yourself.

3. Start keeping a food diary and write down *every single thing you eat and drink.* Even if you're ashamed of something you ate, write it down anyway. This will not only get you in the habit of honestly facing what you're eating, it will remind you to keep your portions small and your fat content low.

    The food diary doesn't have to be anything fancy; most of my clients just buy a little 3 × 5 inch notepad at the grocery store and use one page per day. Keep the diary handy so that you won't forget to write in it. And finally, be sure and write in everything that goes into your mouth, even a glass of water. It's important to keep track of everything to break out of the vicious cycle of sneak-eating.

Closet Chocoholism, once confronted honestly in yourself, is fairly easy to break out of. I've seen many people use a combination of self-honesty and food diaries to comfortably stop sneak-eating. And the good news is that after stopping, most never want to go back.

7

Why You'll Love
This Diet

Now that you've found what style or styles of chocoholism you tend toward, it's time to look at how the actual food you eat will play a role in gaining control over your chocolate cravings. The purpose of The Chocoholic's Dream Diet is twofold:

1. To satisfy your chocolate cravings so you won't feel out of control or deprived.
2. To help you lose weight in a healthy, but steady, manner so that the pounds drop one by one until you reach a weight you feel comfortable with.

The part I find so exciting about The Chocoholic's Dream Diet is that you're able to eat delicious, normal, and easy-to-prepare food *and* have a daily chocolate treat, to boot! It won't feel like you're on a "diet," which implies rules, restrictions, and bland food. Instead, you'll probably find yourself thinking, "I won't possibly be able to lose weight eating all this food and chocolate."

But, as someone who has been through what you're struggling with, I was very careful to plan the diet to maximize your eating pleasure. And, as you may know, when an eating plan is a joy instead instead of a chore, you're more apt to stick with it.

Especially for Chocoholics

As explained in chapters 1 through 6, when chocolate cravings hit, it's usually a lot more than the delicious taste that triggers the appetite. Just by identifying your particular reason for and style of chocoholism, you're already halfway toward learning to control it.

In fact, after first understanding how your personality plays a role in overeating, you may find your appetite for chocolate may temporarily increase. This is normal, and is caused by the anxiety of facing some part of yourself honestly that you may not feel comfortable about.

For instance, Sharon discovered she craved chocolate because of an unsatisfying love relationship she was struggling with. Until she saw her true reason for eating lots of candy bars every day, Sharon hadn't really looked at how unhappy she was in her relationship—she actually didn't want to face it.

When she realized how chocolate was a substitute for the love she was missing, it made Sharon very anxious at first. And *that*, in turn, made her want even more chocolate!

Fortunately, the increased appetite is only temporary, usually a day or two at most. As with other parts of chocoholism, the most important thing for you to do is to stay aware of the connection between your chocolate cravings and your emotional and physical states. By being very honest with yourself about this connection, you'll be less apt to binge in the first place. And if you do happen to go on an eating binge, your self-knowledge will help pull you out of it quickly.

The Physical Nature of Chocoholism

The Chocoholic's Dream Diet isn't just about self-help psychological techniques, however. The actual diet is just as important as self-awareness. There are very real physical reasons why you crave chocolate, as you learned in previous chapters.

When the body becomes depleted of certain vital minerals and amino acids, food cravings begin as a signal, like a fuel light on a car needing gas. With chocolate cravings, the most common depletions are the amino acid tryptophan and the minerals magnesium, chromium, and calcium.

Tryptophan is necessary to create the brain chemical serotonin, which plays a major role in determining your mood and the quality of your sleep. When serotonin becomes depleted, the body signals include chocolate cravings, mood swings, and/or irritability, tiredness, a decreased desire for sex, and insomnia.

Magnesium, chromium, and calcium also play vital roles in your physical and mental health. When you're low on any of these minerals, your energy level drops and you may feel somewhat depressed without really knowing why. Chocolate is craved not only to replenish these minerals, since it contains fairly high amounts of all three, but also because of the desire to get an energy from chocolate's stimulants.

Depletions in tryptophan, magnesium, chromium, and calcium occur because of stress, too stringent dieting, or the menstrual cycle. The Chocoholic's Dream Diet circumvents this physical response by providing a menu high in all four of these vital substances. I think it's important to try and eat a real healthy diet in order to feel and look your best—what's the point of looking slim and trim if you can't enjoy it because you don't feel good?

In addition to the foods outlined in The Dream Diet, I recommend that you take a vitamin/mineral supplement containing magnesium, chromium, and calcium. I have also had great success in treating chocoholics by having them take one 500-milligram L-tryptophan capsule each evening before bedtime. This over-the-counter amino acid pill is available at all drug stores, most department stores, and some grocery stores. It costs approximately six dollars for sixty tablets and is well worth the price—just think what you'll be saving in money previously spent on chocolate!

The Importance of Liquids in The Dream Diet

The liquids you drink can be just as important as the foods you eat when you're dieting or trying to maintain your weight. Many dieters—and especially chocoholics because of their tendency to abuse psychoactive (mood-altering) chemicals in ordinary foods—drink too much diet cola.

The reason I say "too much" is because diet or regular cola, if consumed in too great quantity, makes dieting difficult and even slows weight loss! There are three main problems with drinking diet colas while you're trying to lose weight:

1. A 12-ounce can of diet cola contains 70 milligrams of sodium. This may not seem high when you consider that the average dieting woman should be consuming around 1,000 milligrams of sodium a day. However, just consider this: If you drink four sodas a day, that's 280 milligrams

of sodium! And when you add that sodium to all the salt you normally consume in food, you can easily exceed the 1,000-milligram-per-day level.

Besides being linked to high blood pressure, the foremost concern about sodium for dieters is that it causes water retention. Dieters struggling with weight plateaus often have to cut their diet cola consumption down to a maximum of two cans a day before weight loss can continue.

2. Colas contain about as much caffeine as a half cup of coffee. The caffeine in colas is made from kola nut extract, and regulations keep the caffeine content at a maximum of 0.02 percent of the soda.

However, when dieters drink a great deal of soda (over two cans per day), the caffeine amount accumulates and the result can be a feeling of being nervous, excited, jittery, or anxious. Also, one of the amino acids in the sweetener aspartame (NutraSweet brand sweetener), called phenylalanine, has properties which make some individuals feel anxious.

The resulting tension from caffeine and phenylalanine can trigger a desire to overeat, as the dieter seeks to calm down through the use of food.

3. Cola can reduce your magnesium levels, thereby triggering chocolate cravings. A study conducted by Kenneth Weaver, M.D., at the East Tennessee State University, found that phosphoric acid in cola binds with magnesium in the body and extracts the latter. Each 12-ounce can of cola contains 36 milligrams of phosphoric acid, and

the result is that 36 milligrams of magnesium are removed from the body.

It's important for chocoholics, therefore, to cut down or eliminate the consumption of soda. If you feel you can't live without diet cola, then limit your intake to two cans or 24 ounces a day.

The ideal drink for dieters, as you undoubtedly know, is water. I recommend drinking at least one-half gallon a day, and this can sound like a lot, to be sure. What really works for me, as well as my patients, is to get in the habit of having one-gallon bottles of purified water around at all times to serve as a reminder to drink water. Buy several bottles at the store (they're not all that expensive, especially compared to the price of cola), and carry one to work with you each day.

Water helps dieters for several reasons:

- It makes you feel full, so you won't be as hungry.
- It is actually more energizing than a cup of coffee, so you won't be as apt to reach for a sugary food to try and pep yourself up.
- It flushes salt out of the body, thereby reducing water retention.
- It also flushes out the residuals of burned body fat, a form of ash that remains in the body unless it is flushed out with water.

I've found that the feeling of being deprived about drinking "plain old boring water" is removed by making the water a special drink. Two easy ways to do this are to pour the water into a special, pretty glass and to garnish it with a slice of lemon or lime.

*   *   *

With its combination of psychological and physiological principles, The Chocoholic's Dream Diet will ease, and in many cases erase, your uncomfortable cravings for chocolate.

II

The Chocoholic's Dream Diet

8

The Chocoholic's Dream Diet

It's time to begin your eating plan on The Dream Diet, and while it's a diet that's simple and easy to follow—as well as enjoyable with its daily chocolate snack—it's important to keep some general nutritional information in mind.

The First Important Point: Using The Dream Diet

The aim of this diet is to help you lose weight, maintain optimum physical and mental health, and gain control over your chocolate cravings. *The first important point, then, is to use the portions specified in this chapter to keep your calorie and fat counts low enough to lose weight at a moderate, but satisfying, rate.* If you eat too many, or too few, calories, your body's metabolism won't operate in the most efficient manner and you won't lose weight steadily.

You may already know that habitual dieters—those whose weight fluctuates—have actually trained their bodies to hang on to calories when they go on a diet. So, even though he or she could rapidly lose weight as a young teenager, the lifelong dieter finds that each sub-

73

sequent diet takes weight off just a little bit slower. Add to that the natural metabolic slowdown that accompanies the aging process, and you have one frustrated dieter! Conversely, the slow metabolism also means you put weight back on more quickly than the first time you dieted. It just doesn't seem fair, does it?

The Second Important Point: Your Metabolism and Exercise

There are countless dieting schemes which purport to increase the metabolic rate—these books and programs offer special meals, pills, and liquids which, they say, will maximize your metabolism. *The second important point for you to keep in mind is that there are no known permanent solutions for a slow metabolism; however, exercise is a proven way to temporarily boost metabolism.*

The only two things which we know to *temporarily* increase the metabolic rate are exercise and stimulants such as the nicotine in cigarettes. The latter, of course, shouldn't even be viewed as an option for weight control because of the hideous health hazards associated with cigarette and stimulant abuse. Not to mention how these products sap the beauty right out of your skin, hair, and eyes.

Exercise, however, is as close to a dieting miracle cure as you can come. After exercising, your metabolic rate is increased for at least that day. There is some evidence, also, that regular exercise may have a half-life effect—that is, your metabolism from exercising on Tuesday may still continue to be stepped-up on Wednesday.

Along with this second point, then, is the indisputable fact that anyone wanting a toned, de-stressed, and slim body must work at it a bit by exercising. Whenever I tell this to my clients or students, I hear groans. It's as if the word "exercise" transports them back to 8th grade gym class and all the associated feelings of dread that went along with it.

However, and I cannot emphasize this enough, exer-cise is vital to overcoming your chocoholism. This is for a number of different reasons:

1. It reduces stress, and so your serotonin, mineral, and vitamin levels are not as apt to become depleted. This, in turn, decreases or eliminates chocolate cravings.

2. It temporarily increases your metabolic rate, so that, even after decades of dieting, you'll be able to lose weight.

3. It tones the body in ways that dieting alone can't achieve. There's a real difference, after all, between a skinny and a sleek, athletic body.

4. You'll sleep more soundly at night, which will help to keep your brain chemistry at its optimum balance and levels. And this means feeling rested when you awake and more energetic during the day, and reduces the chance you'll turn to choc-olate for an energy boost.

I recommend exercising *at least* four times a week for forty minutes with some exercise that increases your heart rate aerobically. I know this may sound like a lot, but you'll find that by squeezing exercise into your sched-ule, you'll actually have more time in the long run. This is because you'll feel more energetic and the increased oxygen to the brain often results in creative spurts. In other words, most people find they become more cre-ative and efficient at their jobs after beginning an exer-cise program.

The Third Important Point: Choosing Your Foods

So often, on conventional diets, we're made to feel like little children being told what or what not to do. To me, that mind-set is one of the major reasons why diets fail us 90 percent of the time—the 90 percent of Americans who regain their lost weight within two years of dieting aren't failures; the diets are.

On this diet, I'd like you to remember at all times that you are in complete control of what goes in your mouth and therefore on your hips, thighs, and stomach. Every time you pick up a spoon or fork, you are actually choosing what size body you want to have.

On The Chocoholic's Dream Diet, *the third important point is to choose plenty of foods rich in the minerals and amino acids chocoholic's normally crave—chromium, calcium, magnesium, and tryptophan.* So, while you're following the portion allotment outlined in this chapter, be sure and include the following foods rich in the chocoholic minerals and amino acids in your daily diet as much as possible.

Foods Rich in Chromium

DAIRY
  *American cheese, low-fat

MEAT/PROTEIN
  *Clams, hard- or soft-shell
  *Chicken
  *Peanuts, raw or peanut butter

FRUITS/VEGETABLES
  Apple juice
  Plums

    Prunes
    Corn
    Mushrooms
    *Peas
    *Spinach
    Tomatoes

BREADS/STARCHES

Tortillas
*Corn products
*Wheat products

SPICES/MISCELLANEOUS

Thyme (over 1,000 micrograms of chromium in 3½ ounces)
Chili powder
Cloves
Pepper
Coffee, instant
*Cocoa

Foods Rich in Magnesium

DAIRY:

*Nonfat yogurt

MEAT/PROTEIN

*Shrimp
*Tofu

FRUITS/VEGETABLES

*Beet greens
Chard
*Collard greens
*Lima beans
*Parsley
*Spinach

BREADS/STARCHES
Rice bran
*Corn meal
*Rye flour
*Soybean flour

SPICES/MISCELLANEOUS
*Cocoa

Foods Rich in Calcium

DAIRY
*All milk products

MEAT/PROTEIN
*Salmon
*Sardines
*Tofu

FRUITS/VEGETABLES
*Beet greens
Broccoli
*Collard greens
Fennel leaves
Kale
Mustard greens
*Parsley
Rhubarb
*Spinach
Turnip greens

BREADS/STARCHES
*Corn meal
*Oats
*Soybean flour

SPICES/MISCELLANEOUS
Poppy seeds
*Chocolate products

Foods Rich in Tryptophan

(In order for tryptophan in food to produce serotonin [the brain chemical that regulates mood and sleep quality, among other things], it must be accompanied by a carbohydrate. In other words, just eating a dairy or meat product rich in tryptophan will not necessarily increase your serotonin level. You must eat the tryptophan with a carbohydrate; for example, cheese with bread or crackers; cottage cheese with fruit.)

DAIRY
*Cheddar cheese
*Cottage cheese
*Cream cheese
*Parmesan cheese
*Swiss cheese
Eggs
*Milk

MEAT/PROTEIN
*Fish, all varieties (especially halibut and tuna)
Beef, all varieties
Lamb, all varieties
Pork, all varieties
*Peanuts, raw or peanut butter
Poultry, all varieties

FRUITS/VEGETABLES
*Lima beans
*Peas
*Soybeans

BREADS/STARCHES
*Rye flour
*Soybean flour
*Whole wheat flour

SPICES/MISCELLANEOUS

Brewer's yeast

As you may have noticed, a few foods showed up on more than one list and they are marked with an asterisk (*). These are the foods you'd be wise to include in your diet on a frequent (at least three times a week) basis. By eating these foods regularly, you'll feel that much more comfortable as you gain control over your chocolate cravings. The recipes in chapter 9 will give you a better idea about how to put the whole diet together using these foods.

The Chocoholic's Dream Diet

Part of The Dream Diet is based on research conducted by myself and research reported by the University of California at Berkeley, showing that the old myth, "Eat like a king in the morning, a prince at lunchtime, and a pauper at night" is just that—a myth. The study unveiled evidence that as long as you eat at least three times a day, it really doesn't matter if you eat most of your calories right before you go to bed. These calories will not, as previously believed, magically find their way to your hips while you sleep.

This is important to understand: I firmly believe that chocoholics' breakfast should be the smallest meal of the day, their lunch should be slightly larger, and their dinner should be as large and filling as can fit into The Dream Diet calorie/fat counts.

Most people overeat and oversnack in the evening for emotional as well as physical reasons. Feeling stressed after a long day at work, many people use food at night to unwind or to alleviate boredom. But I feel the biggest reason nighttime overeating occurs is because we so often feel hungry after having a small dinner!

As long as you exercise regularly and pay attention to the total day's calories and fat counts, you won't be in any danger of sabotaging your weight-loss goals by eating a large supper. You'll be doing the opposite, because you'll be eliminating the nighttime munchies which could lead to an eating binge.

Here's what The Dream Diet looks like as a daily menu:

The Chocoholic's Dream Diet Daily Menu

BREAKFAST
(200 calories and 2 grams of fat maximum)

Any combination of the following equaling
200 calories and 2 grams of fat:

Fruit, 100 calories, 0 grams fat
Bread, 100 calories, 0 to 2 grams fat
Dairy, 100 calories, 0 to 2 grams fat

LUNCH
(250 calories and 8 grams of fat maximum)

Fruit or vegetables, half serving, 50 calories,
    0 grams fat
Bread, 100 calories, 0 to 2 grams fat
Dairy, 100 calories, 0 to 8 grams fat

MIDDAY SNACK
(50 calories and 0 grams of fat maximum)

Fruit, ½ serving, 50 calories, 0 grams fat

DINNER
(500 calories and 10 grams of fat maximum)

Vegetables, 100 calories, 0 grams fat
Bread, 100 calories, 0 to 2 grams fat

Meat, poultry, or seafood, 200 calories,
   4 to 10 grams fat
Dairy, 100 calories, 0 to 8 grams fat

SNACK
   (150 to 250 calories and 10 grams of fat maximum)

Chocolate snack

Total: 1,150 to 1,250 calories and 28 to 30 grams
of fat

Think of your calorie allotment as money in the
bank—you have an allowance of 1,250 maximum per
day and you'll want to budget it to get the most possible
enjoyment and nutrition out of each calorie. Just like
you wouldn't spend your whole bank account on something foolish, it's important to weigh each eating choice
with the following question in mind: "Is it worth the
calories I'm eating to consume this?"

Helen was accustomed to denying any knowledge
of calorie counts when she ate or drank. "I'd try to fool
myself by not thinking about how many calories were in
the foods I was eating," she remembered. Like many
people, Helen would rationalize or lie to herself about
the foods she'd eat.

On The Chocoholic's Dream Diet, it's vital that you
keep your eyes wide open at all times and remember
that you, and only you, will pay with weight gains or
plateaus if you go over your 1,250-calorie-a-day allowance. Just as the bank charges overdraft penalties if you
bounce a check, so your body penalizes you for going
over your calorie allowances with extra pounds on the
scale.

If, like Helen, you're used to putting your head in the
sand when it comes to paying attention to calorie counts,

it's time to stop. The Chocoholic's Dream Diet doesn't require you to count each and every calorie down to the last one, but it does ask you to be aware *in general* of which foods contain the most calories. And then avoid those foods.

In addition to your 1,250-calorie daily savings account, you have a daily *fat* spending allowance of 30 grams of fat (making this diet very low in fat at 25 percent fat calories per day). As with spending calories, you'd be wise to spend your fat allowance in the most prudent manner possible. This means trying to keep your fat calories as much in the unsaturated, polyunsaturated, and monosaturated categories as possible.

When cooking, use canola oil (marketed as Puritan Oil) or safflower oil, because they have the lowest saturated fat percentage of any oil available. Olive oil—I prefer the "light" variety because it tastes better to me—is another good choice in cooking, because it's monosaturated fat content is helpful in reducing serum cholesterol.

It is important to keep saturated fat, the kind that raises serum cholesterol, to a minimum in your diet. This fat primarily comes from animal fats, tropical oils such as palm oil, palm kernel oil, and hydrogenated fats such as coconut oil.

Especially interesting to chocoholics is a 1978 study conducted by David Kritchevsky, Ph.D., at the University of Pennsylvania about the effects of the fat in chocolate on serum cholesterol. The study backed up other research which showed that the stearic acid in chocolate may offset, or cancel out, the saturated fat in cocoa butter. In other words, the fat in chocolate behaves differently from fat from other sources. The stearic acid in chocolate "rescues" the serum cholesterol before the cocoa butter has a chance to raise it.

Remember, denying or rationalizing the existence of fat and calories in the food you're eating won't keep the weight off you. Don't play Scarlett O'Hara and say to yourself, "I'll think about it tomorrow!" because tomorrow is when you'll be angry at yourself for weighing so much.

Have you ever watched the game show *Wheel of Fortune*? If so, you've probably seen contestants spending their winnings on merchandise, and at times you may have thought to yourself, "That's too much money to spend on that prize!" A contestant spending $500 on a ceramic decorative dog may seem like she's crazy to you. You think, "If I were she, I'd put that $500 on a gift certificate and *really* get my money's worth!" Yet, when you spend 500 calories (almost half of your day's budget!) on a cheeseburger, aren't you doing the same thing?

I think that many people who overeat—like those who overspend on *Wheel of Fortune*—are unaware of the value per calorie in foods. In other words, they don't know the difference between a good deal and a rip-off when it comes to calorie and fat counts. Take a close look at the chart below and test your knowledge of the calorie and fat content of these common foods—were you aware how many calories or grams of fat were in these?

I know I used to assume certain foods were "dietetic" and others were "fattening." With this black-and-white thinking, I never bothered to investigate just how many calories were in cheese, for instance. I just automatically assumed that this food was good for me, and, therefore, not fattening. Are there some foods you may be mistakenly thinking are low in calories? Chapter 10 examines this issue further, but for now, take a close look and learn which foods will give you the most for your calorie and fat "dollar."

Get Your Calorie "Money's Worth"

A rose may be a rose to your nose, but where losing weight is concerned, your body definitely knows the difference between calorie and fat counts of similar foods. That's why it's so important to learn which foods have the most and least fat in them; what you don't know about a food *can* put the weight on you.

It's not enough to think of certain categories of food—fish, for example—as being dietetic, and others—like beef—as being fattening. *Within* each food category, there are some items loaded with calories and others low in calories. For instance, in the fish category, a 5-ounce portion of sole has 100 calories and less than 1 gram of fat. Does this mean all fish is a diet food? Definitely not! Just look at how many calories salmon has in the same 5-ounce portion: 310 with 19 grams of fat! And rainbow trout and bluefish have almost as many calories.

That's why it's important to learn which items *within* food categories are calorie-laden and which are calorie-few. The chart below will help you see which items in the different categories are lowest in fat and calories. It might be a good idea to photocopy this chart, or just take this book along with you as you learn the values in different foods.

But to start with, there are some rules of thumb to guide you when you're trying to decide what to eat. First, remember to "eat light." The lighter shades of meats, fish, and cheeses generally have the least amount of fat in them, making them lower in calories. Red meats such as beef and pork have more fat than white meats such as chicken and turkey breasts. Also, red fish such as mackerel and salmon are oily and higher in fat than white fish such as halibut and sole. The only cases where you should shy away from the color white in foods are:

1. Avoid the white around beef; this is pure fat or "marble."
2. Avoid white sauces and dressings, unless they are specifically made in a low-fat way. For example, regular blue cheese dressing can have up to 90 calories and 8 grams of fat in a mere tablespoon (and, truthfully, how many of us just put *one* tablespoon of dressing on our salads?). Low-calorie blue cheese dressing, on the other hand, contains between 10 and 15 calories and almost no fat per tablespoon.

With that in mind, try to learn which foods give you the most of your calorie and fat budget.

CALORIE AND FAT CONTENT COMPARISON AND PORTION CHART

This chart shows how many calories and grams of fat are in common foods. Next to each food category (e.g., "Cheese," "Beef," etc.) the calorie and fat allowance for a portion on The Chocoholic's Dream Diet is given. Underneath each category is a list of foods and the weight or size that constitutes a portion. When making a portion, it's vital to pay attention to both fat content and calories. In some cases, such as the oily fish and fatty meats, the fat content is so high that the portion is very small to keep the fat count down. In other words, sometimes you'll be eating fewer calories than the portion allows, just to keep the fat count in line.

Food	Calories	Grams of Fat

Bread, Cereal and Starch Products
(One bread portion equals a maximum of 100 calories and 2 grams of fat)

BREAD AND CEREAL

Bagel, ½	80	1
*Biscuit or roll, 1	65	2
Bread, 1 slice	60–70	1

*This is for plain biscuits made with refined or whole wheat. It does not include buttermilk or prebuttered biscuits because they are too high in fat.

(Whole wheat, mixed grain, or rye; calorie count will vary with brands)

Bread crumbs, ¼ cup	90	1
Bread sticks, 4 sticks	95	1
Cereal, ready to eat	100	2

(Consult package to find 100 calorie/2 fat gram portions, stick with whole grain, low/no-sugar, and low-sodium cereals)

Crackers, 3	60–90	1–2

(Wheat or rye, low-sodium; calorie/fat count will vary with brands)

Croutons, 1 ounce	100	1
English muffin, ½	75	0.5
Muffin, 1 small or ½ large	100	2

(Oat bran or whole wheat)

Food	Calories	Grams of Fat
Noodles, enriched, 1 ounce dry	100	1
Tortilla, 1 corn, without lard	70	1
Tortilla, 1 flour, without lard	95	2

STARCHY VEGETABLES

Corn, 4-inch corn on the cob	100	1
Corn, canned, 1 cup	100	1
Corn, frozen, ½ cup	90	1
Potato, 1 medium	95	0
Rice, ½ cup cooked	100	0

Dairy Products
(One dairy portion equals a maximum of 100 calories and 8 grams of fat)

CHEESE

American, .9 ounce	100	8
American, low-fat, 1.8 ounces	100	4
Blue, 1 ounce	100	8
Brick, .95 ounce	100	8
Brie, 1 ounce	95	8
Camembert, 1 ounce	85	7
Cheddar, .85 ounce	100	8
Colby, .9 ounce	100	8
Cream cheese, .8 ounce	80	8
Edam	100	8
Mozzarella, part-skim, 1.4 ounces	100	7
Parmesan, .9 ounce	100	7
Swiss, 1 ounce	95	7

MILK AND MILK PRODUCTS
(All values are for 1-cup portions)

Buttermilk, 1 cup	100	2
Cottage cheese, ½ cup	100	2

Food	Calories	Grams of Fat
Low-fat cottage cheese, ⅔ cup	100	1
Low-fat milk, 1 cup	100	3
Low-fat plain yogurt, ⅔ cup	100	2
Nonfat milk, 1 cup	90	0.5
Nonfat plain yogurt, ¾ cup	100	0
Whole milk, ¾ cup	100	7
Whole-milk plain yogurt, ½ cup	90	3.5

Fruits

(One Fruit Portion equals a maximum of 100 calories and 0 grams of fat)

Food	Calories	Grams of Fat
Apple, 1 medium	80	0
Apricots, 6 medium	100	0
Banana, 1 medium	100	0
Berries:		
Blackberries, 1⅓ cups	100	0
Blueberries, 1¼ cups	100	0
Boysenberries, 1⅓ cups	90	0
Raspberries, 1½ cups	90	0
Strawberries, 2 cups	90	0
Cantaloupe, 1¾ cups	100	0
Cherries, 20	100	0
Grapefruit, 1 medium	80	0
Grapes, 1⅔ cups	100	0
Guava, 2 medium	90	0
Honeydew melon, small, ¾	100	0
Kiwifruit, 2 medium	100	0
Lemons, 5 medium	100	0
Mango, medium, ¾	100	0
Nectarines, medium, 1½	100	0
Oranges, medium 1½	100	0
Papaya, medium, ¾	90	0
Peaches, 2 medium	75	0
Pear, 1 medium	100	0

Food	Calories	Grams of Fat
Persimmons, 3 medium	100	0
Pineapple, 1¼ cups	100	0
Plums, 2 medium	70	0
Pomegranate, 1 medium	100	0
Tangelos, 2 medium	80	0
Tangerines, 2 medium	80	0
Watermelon, 2 cups	100	0

Meats, Poultry, and Seafood
(One meat portion equals a maximum of 200 calories and 10 grams of fat)

BEEF
(All values are for cooked portions*)

Chuck steak, 1⅓ ounces	120	9
Hamburger, lean, 3 ounces	140	3.5
Porterhouse steak, lean, 2⅓ ounces	160	10
Round steak, lean, 3 ounces	185	4.5
Sirloin steak, lean, 3 ounces	170	9
T-bone steak, lean, 2¼ ounces	155	10

FISH AND SEAFOOD
(All values are for uncooked portions)

Bass, 6 ounces	180	5
Bluefish, 6 ounces	200	6
Butterfish (northern), 3 ounces	145	9
Catfish, 6 ounces	180	5
Clams (meat only), 8 ounces	145	4
Cod, 9 ounces	130	1
Crab legs (meat only), 9 ounces	160	4
Flounder, 10 ounces	200	3
Haddock, 9 ounces	195	9
Halibut, 7 ounces	200	3.5

*Please see note for Pork section, p. 92.

Food	Calories	Grams of Fat
Lobster (meat only), 7 ounces	190	5
Mackerel, 3 ounces	165	10
Perch, 7 ounces	190	2
Rainbow trout, 3 ounces	170	9.5
Red snapper, 7 ounces	190	2
Salmon, 2.5 ounces	155	9.5
Scallops (meat only) 8 ounces	190	3
Sole, 10 ounces	200	10
Swordfish, 5.5 ounces	190	6
Tuna, canned, with water, 6 ounces	190	2
Tuna, yellowfin, 5 ounces	190	4

LAMB
(All values are for cooked portions)

Arm chop, lean, 3½ ounces	180	7
Blade chop, lean, 2⅔ ounces	170	8.5
Loin chop, lean, 3 ounces	160	6.5
Rib chop, lean, 3 ounces	180	7.5

MISCELLANEOUS MEAT-GROUP ITEMS
(These foods are counted into the meat group because they are rich in protein and because they work well as meat substitutes in meal preparation)

Beans		
Garbanzo, 3¾ ounces	190	4
Kidney, 6 ounces	200	1
Lima, 10 ounces	190	0.5
White, ⅔ cup	160	0.5
Egg, 1 large*	80	6

*This food is listed only for your information; it is recommended that you eat or bake with egg substitutes or egg whites (2 egg whites = 1 egg). Eggs are too high in cholesterol to be included in a diet, especially when such easy and delicious substitutes are around.

Food	Calories	Grams of Fat
Egg substitute, .50 ounce (Depending on brand)	60–120	1–6
Peanuts, raw, ¾ ounce	115	9
Tofu, 8 ounces	165	10

PORK
(All values are for cooked portions**)

Bacon, ½ ounce (thin/lean slices)	75	8.5
Blade cut, lean, 1 ounce	110	8.5
Ham, 1.5 ounces (lean/fat-reduced)	130	8
Loin chop, lean, 1 ounce	100	7.5
Sausage, ½ ounce	110	10
Spareribs, ½ ounce	100	9

POULTRY
(All values are for cooked portions)

Chicken, 3.5 ounces (Dark meat, without skin)	200	9
Chicken, 2 ounces (Dark meat, with skin)	130	8
Chicken, 4.5 ounces (Light meat, without skin)	200	4

**In general, I've found that people who eat the "red" meats, beef and pork, more than twice a week have a difficult time losing weight. I've had a substantial number of clients struggle with weight plateaus until they eliminated or radically reduced their intake of red meats—even though their total daily calorie and fat total didn't change substantially.

The high saturated-fat content of beef and pork, to me, just make them a poor "buy" for your calorie and fat "allowance." Why settle for 1⅓ ounces of chuck steak, which carries 9 grams of fat, when you can have a generous 4½ ounces of skinned light-meat chicken with only 4 grams of fat? And with fish, of course, you get even more for your calorie and fat "dollars."

Food	Calories	Grams of Fat
Chicken, 3.5 ounces (Light meat, with skin)	180	7
Duck, without skin, 3 ounces	170	9
Duck, with skin, 1 ounce	95	8
Pheasant, without skin, 5 ounces	190	5.5
Turkey, 3.5 ounces (Dark meat, without skin)	190	7
Turkey, 3 ounces (Dark meat, with skin)	190	10
Turkey, 4.5 ounces (Light meat, without skin)	200	4
Turkey, 3.5 ounces (Light meat, with skin)	195	8.5

Vegetables

(One vegetable portion equals a maximum of 100 calories and 0 grams of fat, all values are for uncooked portions)

Food	Calories	Grams of Fat
Alfalfa sprouts, 8½ ounces	100	0
Artichokes, 2 large	90	0
Asparagus, pieces, 3 cups	100	0
Beets, 4 medium	90	0
Beet greens, 14 ounces	100	0
Bell peppers, 4 large	100	0
Broccoli, 10.5 ounces (Approximately 3 stalks)	100	0
Brussels sprouts, 1½ cups	90	0
Cabbage, shredded, 4 cups	100	0
Carrots, 2 large	85	0
Cauliflower, pieces, 4 cups	100	0
Celery, 12 stalks	100	0
Chard, 14 ounces	100	0
Collard greens, 7½ ounces	100	0
Eggplant, diced, 2 cups	100	0
Fennel leaves, 12¼ ounces	100	0

Food	Calories	Grams of Fat
Kale, 9⅓ ounces	100	0
Lettuce, 27 ounces	100	0
Mushrooms, 35 small	100	0
Mustard greens, 11 ounces	100	0
Okra, cut, 2 cups	100	0
Onions, 2½ medium	95	0
Parsley, 7 ounces	90	0
Peas, ¾ cup	85	0
Radishes, 55 small	95	0
Rhubarb, 3 cups	90	0
Scallions, 10 medium	90	0
Spinach, 14 ounces	100	0
Squash:		
Acorn, ½ medium	90	0
Summer, 2½ cups	100	0
Winter, ¾ cup	95	0
Zucchini, 3 cups	100	0
Tomatoes, 4 small	95	0
3 medium	100	0
2 large	90	0
Turnip greens, 12¼ ounces	100	0
Yellow (wax) beans, 2½ cups	100	0

In the next chapter, you'll find a sample menu plus recipes so you can clearly see how The Chocoholic's Dream Diet works.

A Word about Chocolate Snacks

It's very important for you to include a daily chocolate snack in your diet to keep your cravings tamed to a manageable level. All chocoholics should find that by choosing the *correct* type of chocolate, they'll feel in control (as opposed to wanting to go on a binge) when eating the chocolate snack.

How do you find out the correct type of chocolate for yourself? Well, many people already know that they always binge on chocolate containing refined sugar and, in some cases, corn syrup. These people, as well as Chocolate Bingers, who were identified as sugar bingers in chapter 4, should abstain from all forms of refined sugar in their chocolate. Chocolate Bingers, as mentioned in chapter 4, should also avoid corn syrup. Chapters 10 and 11 give dozens of examples of sugar-free chocolate products you can make or buy.

If you find you only binge on chocolate occasionally, then you'll probably find your problem has been twofold in the past:

1. Having a mind-set which considers chocolate a bad or forbidden food. (Once you've eaten chocolate, you think, "Well, I've blown my diet. Might as well eat some more chocolate.") The truth, of course, is that chocolate isn't a "bad" food. It isn't necessarily all that fattening, either. It's just when we eat *too much* of it that we get into caloric trouble.
2. Binging in response to one of the Chocoholism styles outlined in chapters 1 through 6.

If you are a style other than a Chocolate Binger, then you can have chocolate with refined sugar in it under a couple of important conditions:

1. You keep your portions in line with the lists in chapters 10 and 11 so that they fit into The Dream Diet.
2. During your susceptible times (such as Seasonal Chocoholics during wintertime, or Monthly Cyclic

Chocoholics during their period), have only the chocolate snacks which are extremely low in calories and fat (see chapters 10 and 11), so you can eat quite a lot and really satisfy your chocolate cravings.

Also, during your weak moments when you feel like a binge, it's important to buy or make your chocolate snacks only *one at a time.* That way, if you want to binge (which is still really unlikely once The Dream Diet is under way), you'll have to go through some time and trouble in order to get more chocolate. And that could give you enough time to catch yourself before you binge.

Remember that in the end nothing tastes as good as thin feels. Really!

9

Mealtime Recipes

In this chapter, you'll get a clearer picture of how to put The Chocoholic's Dream Diet into action. The daily menu on pages 81–82 and the recipes here are suggestions only; as long as you follow the diet outlined in chapter 8, you can eat a wide variety of foods.

To begin your diet, you might want to use the daily menu to give you clear guidance about the amount of food to eat at each meal. Once you get in the habit of eating this amount—and it will feel like a lot of food, since the calories are spread out differently from most diets—you'll be able to continue The Dream Diet with your own recipes or at restaurants.

Pick one meal from the breakfast, lunch, and dinner categories. Between lunch and dinner, have a 50-calorie fruit snack (see the list in chapter 8). And after dinner, be sure and have your chocolate snack as outlined in chapter 8 and chapters 10 and 11.

Breakfast Recipes

COCOA-HONEY BRAN MUFFINS
Makes 8 muffins
(131 calories and 0.5 grams of fat each)

1 cup oat bran
½ cup egg substitute
½ cup nonfat milk
5 tablespoons frozen concentrated unsweet-
    ened apple juice
1 tablespoon cocoa powder
2 tablespoons honey

Mix all the ingredients, except the honey, by hand in a large bowl; the batter will be slightly lumpy. Pour the batter into a shallow microwaveproof cake pan or eight sections of a microwaveproof muffin pan.

Cook in the microwave oven on medium for 15 minutes, turning two or three times during the cooking process. Remove from the microwave oven and spread the honey over the top of the cake or muffins. Return to the microwave oven and cook for 3 minutes on high.

If cooking in a cake pan instead of a muffin pan, remove from the microwave oven and cut the cake into eight equal pieces. Return to the microwave oven and cook for an additional 2 minutes on high. Muffins will be moist while warm; firmer after refrigeration.

CHOLESTEROL-FREE
EGGS AND BACON
Serves 2
(115 calories and 4 grams of fat per serving)

½ cup egg substitute
4 bacon-style breakfast strips (such as
    Morningstar Farms or another cholesterol-
    free brand)
1 medium orange

Pour the egg substitute into a nonstick frying pan and
heat over low heat, stirring frequently. Cook until a scrambled
egg texture is achieved.

Cook the breakfast strips as directed on the package
(usually microwave cooking for several minutes is required).

Peel the orange and section it in half. One serving
equals one half of the scrambled eggs, two breakfast strips,
and one half of the orange.

GARDEN OMELET ALFRESCO
Serves 1
(130 calories and 2.3 grams of fat)

1 small unpeeled zucchini, sliced
1 scallion, diced
⅛ teaspoon ground pepper
½ small tomato or 6 cherry tomatoes, sliced
⅛ teaspoon oregano
⅛ teaspoon marjoram
¼ cup egg substitute
½ ounce park-skim mozzarella cheese, grated
    or sliced

Place all the ingredients, except the egg substitute
and mozzarella cheese, in a microwaveproof bowl. Mix
and cover. Cook in the microwave oven for 5 minutes on
high.

Pour the egg substitute over the vegetables and cover Cook for 2 minutes in the microwave oven on high. Sprinkle the mozzarella cheese over the top of the omelet and cover Cook for 1 minute more on high and serve.

FRUIT AND
COTTAGE CHEESE SALAD
Serves 1
(Approximately 140 to 150 calories, depending on topping and 1 gram of fat)

2 large leaves lettuce
½ cup low-fat cottage cheese
One of the following fruit toppings:
    ½ cup fruit salad or pineapple chunks
    packed in juice
    1 cup fresh berries
    1 medium apple, sliced and sprinkled with
        cinnamon
    1 large kiwifruit, sliced
    1 large fresh peach, sliced

Arrange the lettuce leaves on a plate or in a bowl an scoop the cottage cheese on top. Using the back of a spoon press an indentation into the cottage cheese to act as "bowl" for the fruit. Put the fruit on the cottage cheese.

WHITE RICE CEREAL
Serves 1
(145 calories and less than 1 gram of fat)

½ cup cold cooked white rice (prepared the
    night before)
½ cup nonfat milk
2 Equal packets (NutraSweet brand sweetener)

Put the rice in a small bowl and add the milk and Equal Eat as you would a prepared cold cereal. Delicious!

FRESH BERRY YOGURT
Serves 1
(150 calories and less than one gram of fat)

1 cup plain nonfat yogurt
1 cup fresh berries, such as strawberries, blue-
    berries, boysenberries, or a combination
2 Equal packets

Put the yogurt into a bowl and add the fruit and Equal.
Stir together and enjoy!

COLD CEREAL AND MILK
Serves 1
(Approximately 145 calories and 0 grams of fat, depending on type of cereal used)

1 ounce (approximately ¾ cup) whole-grain
    cereal with no sugar added (such as Nutri-
    Grain brand cereal)
½ cup nonfat milk

As with any cereal prepare by pouring the cereal into a
bowl and covering with the milk.

FRENCH TOAST
Serves 1
(140 calories and 3 grams of fat)

⅛ cup egg substitute
2 tablespoons nonfat milk
⅛ teaspoon sugar-free vanilla extract
1 slice whole wheat toast
1 teaspoon low-calorie margarine
2 teaspoons light corn syrup

Put the egg substitute, milk, and vanilla extract into a
bowl and stir. Soak the toast in the mixture until the liquid is
completely absorbed.

Melt the margarine and corn syrup in a small skillet over low heat. Cook the soaked bread in the skillet for 3 to 4 minutes on each side, or until browned.

BREAKFAST SMOOTHIE
Serves 1
(150 calories and 2 grams of fat)

½ medium banana
½ cup nonfat milk
2 tablespoons wheat germ
½ cup ice cubes

Peel and slice the banana. Place all the ingredients in a blender and blend at medium speed until the ice is completely crushed.

Lunchtime Recipes

VEGETABLE
HUEVOS RANCHEROS
Serves 2
(185 calories and 6 grams of fat each)

4 scallions
1 zucchini
1 cup broccoli florets
10 mushrooms
2 ounces part-skim mozzarella cheese
3 tablespoons chunky salsa
2 packages egg substitute equivalent to 4 eggs

Dice or slice the vegetables and grate the cheese, then set aside.

In a nonstick skillet, heat the salsa over low heat for 1 minute. Add the scallions and stir until sautéed (about 2 minutes). Add the zucchini and broccoli and distribute over the heat evenly, stirring for approximately 2 minutes. Next, add the mushrooms and stir briefly. Turn the heat up to medium setting.

Pour in the egg substitute and stir continuously, bringing the edges into the center to ensure even cooking. When the egg is spongy throughout, remove from the heat. Sprinkle three quarters of the cheese over the omelet, then, using a spatula, fold the omelet over on top of itself to make a half-circle shape. Sprinkle the remaining cheese on top. Slice in half to make two servings.

MOCK SOFT TACOS
Serves 1
(180 calories and 4.5 grams of fat)

2 tablespoons low-fat cottage cheese
2 tablespoons low-fat, low-calorie sour
   cream
3 tablespoons salsa, fresh preferred
1 unenriched corn or whole wheat tortilla,
   prepare without lard (vegetarian style)
¼ cup shredded lettuce

Mix the cottage cheese, sour cream, and salsa together in a bowl and set aside.

Cook the tortilla in the microwave oven on high for 5 seconds to heat and soften it. Spoon the cottage cheese mixture into the taco and sprinkle the shredded lettuce over it. Roll into a taco shape and enjoy!

BLT SANDWICH
Serves 1
(240 calories and 2 grams of fat)

  2 bacon-style breakfast strips (such as
    Morningstar Farms or another cholesterol-
    free brand)
  1 tablespoon low-fat, low-calorie mayonnaise
  2 slices whole wheat bread
  2 leaves lettuce
  3 large slices tomato

Cook the breakfast strips in the microwave oven on high until very crisp, according to the directions on the package. Spread the mayonnaise on the bread, and add the breakfast strips, lettuce, and tomato to make a sandwich.

SPICY STEAMED ARTICHOKES
Serves 2
(A filling meal for only 65 calories
and 1 gram of fat per portion)

  2 large artichokes
  4 tablespoons low-calorie blue cheese dressing
  2 tablespoons salsa

Put a steamer basket in the bottom of a large pot and pour enough water into the pot to touch the bottom of the steamer. Put on high heat.

Cut the stems and the two bottom rows of leaves off of each artichoke. Place upside down in the pot and cover. Cook for 5 minutes on high heat, then reduce the heat to low and simmer for 20 minutes. Be careful to check the water level from time to time so that the pot doesn't boil dry.

Blend the salad dressing and salsa together and pour into two separate bowls.

To eat the artichoke, peel off the leaves from the bottom and dip the soft leaf ends into the dressing sauce. Bite and scrape the soft ends into your mouth. The middle of the artichoke can also be dipped into the sauce and enjoyed. (Just be sure to cut off the featherlike flower stems before eating the inside of the artichoke).

CANDIED GARDEN SALAD
Serves 2 generously
(125 calories and .75 grams of fat each)

2 large unpeeled carrots, grated
1 medium unpeeled red apple, diced into
    ¼-by-¼-inch pieces
2 stalks celery, diced
2 tablespoons plain nonfat yogurt
1 tablespoon honey

Place the carrot, apple, and celery pieces in a large bowl. In a separate container, thoroughly blend the yogurt and honey. Pour this dressing over the fruit-and-vegetable mixture and stir so that everything is covered.

Serving suggestion: Serve over lettuce leaves in decorative bowls.

SEAFOOD SALAD TANGO
Serves 3 generously
(167 calories and less than 1 gram of fat)

5 asparagus stocks, sliced
1 cup broccoli florets, diced
1 medium unpeeled red apple, diced
8 ounces imitation crab meat, shredded
1 cup plain nonfat yogurt
5 tablespoons salsa, fresh preferred
1 teaspoon honey

Combine the asparagus, broccoli, apple, and shredded crab meat in a large bowl. In a separate bowl, mix the yogurt, salsa, and honey completely and pour the dressing over the salad.

Blend with a spoon until all of the salad is covered with the dressing. Cover and refrigerate for at least 3 hours to marinate, before serving.

STUFFED ZUCCHINI OLÉ
Serves 4
(61 calories and 1.4 grams of fat each)

4 large zucchini
3 tablespoons low-fat cottage cheese
3 tablespoons chunky salsa
1 ounce part-skim mozzarella cheese

Cut each zucchini in half lengthwise. Do not cut off the ends of the zucchini. Put the zucchini, skin side down, on a microwaveproof plate or pan. Cover and cook in the microwave oven for 10 minutes on high. Allow the zucchini to cool for 2 to 3 minutes before removing.

Using a sharp knife and a large spoon, scoop the pulp out of each zucchini and place the pulp in a mixing bowl. Reserve the skins. Add the cottage cheese and salsa to the pulp and blend with a spoon.

Spoon the mixture into the zucchini skins. Place one slice of mozzarella cheese on each zucchini half. Cover and cook in the microwave oven for 3 minutes on high.

One serving equals two zucchini halves.

CREAM CHEESE QUESADILLA
Serves 1
(190 calories and 7 grams of fat)

1 ounce low-calorie cream cheese
2 tortillas, prepared without lard (vegetarian style)
1 tablespoon salsa

Spread the cream cheese to completely cover one side of 1 tortilla. Spread the salsa over the cream cheese and cover with the second tortilla. Put on a microwaveproof plate and cook in the microwave oven for 2 minutes on high.

MARINATED VEGETABLE SALAD
Serves 2
(100 calories and 6 grams of fat each)

One 16-ounce package frozen chunky mixed
    vegetables (such as baby carrots, broccoli
    florets, and cauliflower florets)
½ cup low-calorie Italian salad dressing

Put the frozen vegetables in a medium-size bowl and
cover with the salad dressing. Allow the vegetables to thaw
and marinate overnight in the refrigerator before serving.

CREAM OF GARDEN
VEGETABLE SOUP
Serves 15
(60 calories and 0.25 grams of fat each)

10 unpeeled carrots, finely diced
1 cup broccoli florets, chopped
2 cups asparagus, chopped
7 stalks celery, diced
25–30 pearl onions, peeled
½ cup fresh cilantro, chopped
1 tablespoon ground black pepper
1 large clove garlic
3 cups nonfat milk
6 cups water

Cook all the ingredients in an uncovered extra-large pot
over low heat for 2 hours, stirring frequently.

CHILLED CHICKEN-FRUIT SALAD
Serves 4
(165 calories and 3 grams of fat each)

    2 chicken breast halves
    4 stalks celery
    1 tablespoon pineapple juice
    2 tablespoons low-fat, low-calorie mayonnaise
    2 tablespoons plain nonfat yogurt
    ¼ teaspoon ground black pepper
    1 cup juice-packed pineapple chunks, drained
    ¼ cup raisins

Remove the skin from the chicken and cook the chicken in a pot of boiling water.

While the chicken is cooking, dice the celery. Mix the pineapple juice, mayonnaise, yogurt, and pepper in a bowl. Fold in the pineapple chunks, celery, and raisins.

When the chicken meat has turned completely white, rinse the chicken in cold water to remove any remaining fat and to cool the temperature of the meat. Cut the chicken into cubes about 1-by-1-inch in size. If the chicken meat is still warm, chill it in the refrigerator briefly. Fold the chicken meat into the salad and serve over lettuce leaves.

TANGY TUNA SALAD
Serves 2
(180.5 calories and 6 grams of fat each)

    ¼ cup egg substitute
    One 6½-ounce can white tuna packed in water
    2 tablespoons low-fat, low-calorie mayonnaise
    1 teaspoon mustard
    ⅛ teaspoon ground black pepper
    ¼ teaspoon salt-free seasoning mix
    ½ medium red tomato

Pour the egg substitute into a microwaveproof bowl and cook in the microwave oven on high for 2½ minutes.

Put in the refrigerator to cool while you prepare the tuna salad.

Drain the tuna and place it in a large mixing bowl. Using a fork, separate the tuna into smaller chunks and flakes. Add the mayonnaise, mustard, pepper, and seasoning mix, and stir well.

Remove the cooked egg substitute from the refrigerator and cut it into small pieces, much like crumbled egg yolk. Stir the egg substitute into the tuna mixture.

Dice the tomato into small pieces and gently fold into the tuna salad. Serve over lettuce leaves.

"LIGHT" STUFFED POTATOES
Serves 4
(100 calories and 1.6 grams of fat each)

4 medium potatoes
4 tablespoons low-fat, low-calorie sour cream
2 tablespoons nonfat milk
1 tablespoon salt-free seasoning mix

Wash the potatoes and pierce the skins with a fork twice. Cook the unpeeled potatoes in the microwave oven on high for 15 minutes. Allow the potatoes to cool at least 10 minutes.

Slice the potatoes in half lengthwise, scoop out the insides (leaving the skins intact), and place the potato whites in a large mixing bowl. Place the skins on a microwaveproof bowl so that they are standing like small potato bowls.

Mash the potatoes with a fork or potato masher and add the sour cream and milk. Blend with a mixer on low speed for 1 minute or until the potatoes have a creamy texture. Add the seasoning mix and blend for an additional 30 seconds.

Scoop the mixture into the potato skins and cook in the microwave oven on high for 5 minutes. One serving equals two potato halves.

Dinner Recipes

LIGHT AND SPICY LASAGNA
Serves 6 generously
(180 calories and 4.25 grams of fat each)

This meal takes about an hour to prepare—relatively quick compared to many Italian dishes. It tastes delicious and isn't far from the flavor of traditional lasagna. In fact, my own children never guessed (until I told them later) that they were eating a low-calorie version of lasagna that had tofu in it.

> 16 ounces lasagna noodles
> Two 15-ounce cans tomato sauce
> 1 medium brown onion, peeled and diced
> 3 large cloves garlic, pressed or diced
> ½ teaspoon rosemary
> ½ teaspoon marjoram
> 1 teaspoon oregano
> 1 package (approximately 14 ounces) tofu
>   (Japanese style, not firm)
> ½ cup low-fat, low-calorie sour cream
> 1½ cups low-fat cottage cheese

In a large pot on a back burner, cook the noodles over high heat.

In a separate large pot, combine the tomato sauce, onion, garlic, and spices. Drain the tofu and slice lengthwise, crosswise, and in half to make small squares (about ¼-by-¼-inch). Add the tofu to the sauce and cook over low-medium heat, stirring frequently. Use the back of a stirring spoon to crush the tofu as you stir.

In a large bowl, combine the sour cream and cottage cheese until both ingredients are thoroughly blended.

When the noodles are mostly cooked (not so soft that they will tear when lifted, but not crisp, either), spoon 3 tablespoons of the lasagna sauce on the bottom of a 9-by-13-inch or 8-by-8-inch microwaveproof pan. Layer the noodles over the sauce, slightly overlapping the edges of the noodles. Make sure the noodles fill the bottom of the pan completely, then spoon the sauce to cover the top of the noodles to about ½-inch thickness.

Next, spoon the cottage cheese mixture over the sauce to about ½-inch thickness. Alternate the remaining ingredients in the same way: noodles, sauce, cheese, etc. Cook the lasagna in the microwave oven for 6 minutes and let sit for about 2 minutes before serving. Slice into six or more pieces.

CALIFORNIA CHICKEN À LA KING
Serves 4
(230 calories and 1.5 grams of fat each)

2 skinless chicken breasts
One 16-ounce package frozen mixed vegetables
2 cups water
2 large cloves garlic, pressed or diced
2 teaspoons salt-free seasoning mix
1 cup uncooked white rice
4 tablespoons low-calorie cream cheese
½ cup nonfat milk

Boil the chicken breasts in a large pot of boiling water until the chicken meat is completely white. Cook the frozen mixed vegetables in the microwave oven or on the stove top, according to package directions. Drain the water completely from the pans containing the vegetables and chicken. Set the vegetables and chicken aside momentarily.

In a medium or large cooking pot, place the 2 cups water, garlic, seasoning mix, and white rice over high heat. Bring to a boil and cover. Turn the heat to the lowest possible setting and let simmer until the water is absorbed, about 15 minutes.

While the rice is cooking, shred the chicken into small (approximately 1-by-½-inch) pieces. When the rice is cooked (soft and fluffy), add the cream cheese and nonfat milk, and stir completely. Gently fold in the chicken pieces and vegetables and serve.

"HONEY-ROASTED" CHICKEN
Serves 2
(207.5 calories and 3 grams of fat each)

2 skinless chicken breast halves
2 tablespoons honey
2 tablespoons salt-free seasoning mix

Place the chicken in a shallow microwaveproof pan. Spread 1 tablespoon of the honey over the top and bottom of each breast and sprinkle the seasoning mix to cover the honey. Cover and cook in the microwave oven for 7 minutes on high. Turn the pan one-half rotation and cook an additional 8 minutes on high.

QUICK AND DELICIOUS JAPANESE CASSEROLE
Serves 2
(308 calories and 6 grams of fat each)

White rice to make 1 cup when cooked
1 tablespoon low-calorie margarine
½ large brown onion, diced
1 clove garlic, diced
1 large carrot, grated
4 scallions (green onions), roots removed,
    sliced in half lengthwise
3 tablespoons low-salt soy sauce
3 tablespoons liquid from tofu package
8 ounces firm (one-half normal-size package)
    Japanese-style tofu, chopped into small
    squares approximately ½-by-½-inch
1 package frozen egg substitute, defrosted, or
    egg whites from two large eggs

Prepare the rice according to package directions. Set aside.

In a large skillet, melt the margarine over low heat. Add the onion and garlic, and sauté until the edges of the onion pieces are lightly browned. Add the grated carrot, the scallions, and 1 tablespoon of the soy sauce. Stir until the carrot and scallions are covered with the mixture.

Add the tofu liquid and tofu squares. Allow the mixture to cook, still on low heat, for 1 minute before stirring to ensure the tofu browning on all sides.

Stir in the rice gently and add the remaining 2 tablespoons of soy sauce. Stir until the entire mixture is golden brown. Add the egg substitute and stir until scrambled throughout the rice and tofu. Spoon into bowls and top each serving with 1 additional teaspoon of low-salt soy sauce.

CHICKEN SUMMER GRILL
Serves 4
(350 calories and 5.5 grams of fat each)

1½ pounds chicken breasts
5 tablespoons salsa
6 carrots
6 zucchini
1 large brown onion

Skin and debone the chicken breasts and slice into small (about 3-by-1-inch) strips. Heat the salsa in a large skillet over medium heat and when the salsa starts to bubble around the edges, add the chicken.

While the chicken is cooking (stir occasionally), slice the carrots, zucchini, and brown onion into thin strips, about 4-inches long. When the chicken turns white throughout, add the vegetables. Reduce the heat to low and cover the skillet, allowing the vegetables to steam-cook from the heat of the chicken. Stir frequently to ensure even cooking. The meal is finished when the carrots are softened.

TOFU VEGETABLE STEW
Serves 3
(245 calories and 3 grams of fat each)

A spicy, low-fat meal that's filling and good.

    4 cups water
    1 medium unpeeled brown potato, cubed
    1 large brown onion, diced
    3 large unpeeled carrots, sliced
    1 large unpeeled Beefsteak tomato, cubed
    1 large clove garlic, pressed or finely diced
    ¼ teaspoon ground black pepper
    1/16 teaspoon cayenne pepper
    ½ package (approximately 8 ounces) tofu,
        cubed into ½-by-½-inch squares
    3 cups cooked white rice

In a nonaluminum pot, bring the water to a boil and gently stir in the remaining ingredients. Simmer on low heat for 2 hours, stirring approximately every half hour. Serve each portion over 1 cup of rice.

HAWAIIAN CHICKEN LUAU
Serves 2
(400 calories and 1.5 grams of fat each)

    White rice to make 1 cup when cooked
    2 chicken breast halves, approximately
        3 ounces each
    1 red bell pepper
    One 20-ounce can pineapple chunks packed
        in juice
    1 tablespoon salt-free seasoning mix
    2 tablespoons low-salt soy sauce

Prepare the rice according to package directions and set aside. Skin and debone the chicken and cut into thin strips. Cut the bell pepper into slices, about 4-by-½-inch in size.

Over medium heat, pour the pineapple chunks and juice into a skillet. Add the chicken, bell pepper, and seasoning mix, and stir until the chicken turns white (about 15 minutes).

Serve over ½ cup rice and top each serving with 1 tablespoon of soy sauce.

SPICY SHRIMP FIESTA
Serves 2
(370 calories and 10 grams of fat each)

2 zucchini
2 summer squash
1 small brown onion or 5 pearl onions
White rice to make 1 cup when cooked
2 ounces part-skim mozzarella cheese
8 ounces hot-flavored salsa
2 cups broccoli florets
½ pound bay shrimp (precooked or uncooked)

Dice the zucchini into coin-shaped pieces, and dice the squash and onion into small pieces, approximately ½-by-½-inch in size. Cook the rice according to package directions and set aside. Grate the cheese and set aside.

In a large skillet, heat the salsa over low heat and add the vegetables. Stir constantly for about 3 minutes and add the shrimp. Turn the heat up to medium and continue to stir another 3 to 4 minutes, making certain all the shrimp is cooked. Turn the heat to low and allow the mixture to cook an additional 2 minutes, stirring once or twice.

Serve the mixture over ½ cup rice per serving and sprinkle the cheese over the top. The cheese can be melted by placing the serving dish in the microwave oven and cooking on high for 1 to 1½ minutes. Delicious and colorful, too!

FISH FAJITAS
Serves 4
(440 calories and 5 grams of fat each, one serving equals 2 fajitas plus ½ cup Spanish rice)

> 7 tablespoons medium to hot salsa, fresh
>   preferred
> 1 cup uncooked white rice
> 2 pounds sole fish
> 1 large onion
> 1 green bell pepper
> 1 tablespoon light olive oil
> 1 large clove garlic
> 3 tablespoons medium to hot taco sauce
> ½ cup plain nonfat yogurt
> 8 tortillas, prepared without lard (vegetarian
>   style)

In a medium saucepan, bring 2 cups of water plus 2 tablespoons of the salsa to a boil. Add the rice and cover. Turn the heat to low and simmer.

Cut the fish, onion, and bell pepper into thin strips, about 5-by-½-inch, and set aside.

Put the olive oil in the bottom of a large skillet and turn the heat to medium. Dice or press the garlic clove into the skillet and stir. Add 3 tablespoons of the salsa and the taco sauce and stir. Put the onion and bell pepper into a pan and stir for about 2 minutes. Gently add the fish and let simmer for 2 minutes before stirring. The fish will slightly break up during the cooking process, but if you exercise care, you'll be able to keep the fish from flaking and completely losing its shape.

While the fish is simmering, check the rice. If the water is almost all absorbed, then turn the heat off and allow the rice to stand—still covered—while you prepare the mock sour cream.

Mock sour cream: Combine ½ cup plain nonfat yogurt with the remaining 2 tablespoons salsa.

To prepare the fajitas, heat the tortillas in the microwave oven on high for about 1 minute in their original plastic bag container (puncture to allow steam to escape). Put one eighth of the fish fajita mixture one each tortilla and add 1 teaspoon of the mock sour cream—this can be eaten by folding the tortilla into a taco shape, or by cutting and eating like a tostada. Serve ½-cup rice with each serving as a side dish.

STUFFED ITALIAN VEGGIES
Serves 4
(80 calories and 0.5 grams of fat each)

This meal is a great way to make vegetables the main dish. Low on calories, this meal is very high on taste and texture. This meal is also extremely filling—after eating one serving, you'll feel stuffed!

    4 large zucchinis
    4 large yellow squash
    4 tablespoons low-fat cottage cheese
    2 tablespoons low-calorie blue cheese dressing
    1 teaspoon oregano
    ¼ teaspoon marjoram
    ¼ teaspoon ground pepper
    ¼ teaspoon salt-free onion powder
    ¼ teaspoon salt-free garlic powder

Leaving the ends intact, cut the zucchini and squash in half lengthwise. Place on a microwaveproof plate or dish and cover. Microwave on high for 10 minutes. Let cool, then scoop out the middle of the zucchini and squash, using a knife and spoon. Place the pulp in a blender, and add the remaining ingredients.

Blend on low speed for 30 seconds. Pour the mixture into the zucchini and squash skins. Heat in the microwave oven on high for 2 minutes.

One serving equals 2 zucchini halves and 2 squash halves.

SEAFOOD KABOBS
Serves 4
(310 calories and 6.5 grams of fat each serving)

MARINADE:

  ⅓ cup light olive oil
  ⅓ cup white or blush wine
  ⅓ cup seasoned rice vinegar (Japanese style)
  1 tablespoon salt-free seasoning mix

KABOBS:

  1 pound medium or large uncooked shrimp
  1 pound small or medium uncooked bay
    scallops
  1 large brown onion
  1 large green bell pepper
  1 red bell pepper
  3 large zucchini
  3 yellow squash
  15 cherry tomatoes

Mix the ingredients in the marinade recipe together thoroughly and set aside.

Peel and devein the shrimp and place it in a large bowl with the scallops. Pour one half of the marinade (if the marinade has settled, be sure to stir before pouring it) over the shrimp and scallops. Put in the refrigerator and stir occasionally. The fish should marinate for at least 1 hour.

Slice all the vegetables except the tomatoes into bite size pieces (about 1-by-1-inch). Put all the vegetables into a large bowl and pour the remaining marinade over them.

After the fish and vegetables have soaked for at least 1 hour, skewer them with wooden or metal kabob skewers. Put all the scallops together and all the shrimp together on skewers. The vegetables should go on skewers separately from the fish, and the meal looks best if you alternate the vegetables (for instance, first a cherry tomato, next an onion wedge, followed by a bell pepper slice, etc.).

Place the fish and vegetable kabobs on a pan and cook in a preheated broiler for 3 minutes. Turn everything over once and cook an additional 2 minutes.

One serving equals one fourth of the fish and vegetable skewers.

TOFU-STUFFED BELL PEPPERS
Serves 6
(345 calories and 9 grams of fat each)

2 cups uncooked white rice
4 cups water
3 teaspoons paprika
2 teaspoons salt-free onion powder
3 large cloves garlic, diced
1 tablespoon extra-light olive oil
1 package tofu (approximately 14 ounces)
¼ teaspoon ground pepper
6 large green bell peppers
6 ounces part-skim mozzarella cheese

Put the rice, water, 2 teaspoons of the paprika, and onion powder into a large pot. Bring to a boil over high heat. Cover and turn the heat down to the lowest possible setting.

In a nonstick skillet, sauté the garlic in the olive oil over low heat. Drain the tofu and cut into small (approximately ½-by-½-inch) pieces. Add the tofu, the remaining 1 teaspoon of paprika, and the ground pepper to the garlic. Stir until the mixture turns red-orange from the paprika.

Cut the tops off each bell pepper and remove the seeds from the inside. Next, grate the cheese.

Stuff the bell peppers by alternating layers of cheese and rice mixture until each pepper is full, with rice as the top layer. Save 1 ounce of the cheese to top the peppers later. Cook the peppers in the microwave oven for 10 minutes on high. Turn the pan one rotation and cook an additional 10 minutes on high.

Put the remaining cheese on top of each pepper and sprinkle with paprika. Return the peppers to the microwave oven and cook for 1½ minutes on high, or until the cheese topping melts.

How to Eat Out—
and Stay With the Plan

These recipes can also serve as guidelines for ordering meals at restaurants. To me, eating out is both a necessity and a pleasure. As with most people who juggle career and family, I often eat at all sorts of places: fast-food joints, airplanes, friends' houses, and hotels. And I've learned I can eat anywhere in any city and still eat a healthful, low-calorie meal—if I plan ahead a bit.

For example, when eating breakfast away from home, many people are tempted to eat an all-American special, complete with syrupy pancakes, buttery eggs, greasy hash browns, and fat-laden bacon. What else can you eat for breakfast at restaurants? I recommend you order a fresh fruit salad with cottage cheese or plain yogurt (usually on the lunch or dinner menu). Make sure the fruit is either fresh or juice-packed and don't eat any fruit canned with sugary syrup. Also be sure to ask the waiter for low-fat cottage cheese.

Other restaurant breakfast ideas include corn flakes topped with fresh fruit and low-fat or skim milk or a glass of orange juice with whole wheat toast and a soft-boiled egg. Of course, you'll want to skip the butter for the toast and use the yolk of the egg instead.

Lunchtime is probably the most difficult for "working dieters" because it's so tempting to overeat or to eat high-fat foods during a rushed lunch hour. Brown-bagging a lunch for work requires a great deal of planning and preparation—something that is nonetheless necessary for successful weight loss and maintenance.

Bring a lunch to work is the ideal way to stay in control of your eating. You'll also reduce your stress level if you *make* the time each evening to prepare a lunch (such as a colorful salad or a sandwich made with whole wheat bread, lean turkey breast, mustard, romaine lettuce, and tomato slices). One client of mine even decided to lay out her clothes for the next day, as well as prepare her lunch, each evening before going to bed. As a result, she was able to sleep in an extra fifteen minutes in the morning instead of having to rush around finding something to wear or making lunch at the last minute.

Eating lunch out, though, doesn't have to mean eating high-fat. In fact, since the meals for dinner and lunch are so similar, I've listed some suggestions for different types of restaurants:

American—Salads (avoid cheese and high-fat meat toppings) ordered with low-calorie dressing on the side. You can dip each bite of salad into the dressing and end up using a lot less dressing and fewer calories. Also, grilled or steamed fish and poultry, served with steamed rice and lightly seasoned vegetables.

Italian—my favorite is an antipasto salad (without any meat) because I love the variety of beans and peppers served with fresh vegetables. A pasta dish topped with a meatless tomato or pesto sauce is also a good alternative.

Mexican—Choose a chicken tostada (salad), but definitely ask that it be prepared without refried beans (these contain lard, a form of almost pure saturated fat!). Also, avoid the fried tortillas, sour cream, and guacamole, because these are also high in fat. Another

Mexican favorite of mine is fajitas—grilled chicken or shrimp with onions and bell peppers.

Oriental—Chinese, Japanese, and Thai foods are all unique, reflecting the individualities of their respective countries; however, some generalities about the healthfulness of Oriental food can be drawn. Most Oriental food is based on lightly cooked vegetables, low-fat meats, and steamed rice. For this reason, Oriental restaurants are an excellent choice for the weight-conscious. It's easier to suggest what *not* to eat in these places: sweet and sour dishes (high in sugar and corn syrup); MSG and high-sodium soy sauce (most places are more than happy to prepare dishes without MSG and offer reduced-sodium soy sauce); fried foods such as crispy noodles and egg rolls.

Fast food, lunch wagons, delis, and cafeterias—These eateries are almost synonymous with fat-laden foods, and caution on your part can make the difference between a 350-calorie and a 2000-calorie meal. Avoiding fried foods—hamburgers, chicken patties and nuggets, fried fish sandwiches, onion rings, and french fries—is foremost, of course. Fortunately, most eateries now offer salads and salad bars—Just stay away from high-fat dressings and cheeses. I've also had delis make me salads from their sandwich makings: lettuce, tomato, and some low-fat turkey strips make a delicious meal. Lunch wagons and cafeterias also usually serve another of my favorite lunches: a large tomato stuffed with chicken salad.

Eating out doesn't need to be a worrisome experience. With a little preparation (for example, phoning ahead to a restaurant to see if they offer grilled fish and other healthful entrées) and caution (such as asking the waiter to prepare the food to your specifications), you can dine at restaurants regularly and still see progress in your fitness program.

10

Delicious Sugar-Free Chocolate Dessert and Drink Recipes

Please don't be afraid to try some of these recipes for chocolate. Even if you've never really tried cooking before, if you follow the easy directions, you'll soon find yourself cooking like a professional!

The chocolate desserts are divided into categories based upon their sweetening agent. Since none of these recipes uses refined sugar, all styles of Chocoholics will be able to use these desserts without feeling as if they want to binge.

The calorie and fat content per portion is listed with each recipe to make it easy for you to see how to fit these desserts into your daily chocolate snack time. Remember that The Chocoholic's Dream Diet allows you to have one chocolate snack each evening with a maximum of 250 calories and 10 grams of fat.

As you're eating your chocolate, be sure to do everything possible to maximize your pleasure. Avoid distractions such as television, reading, driving, or even talking. Instead, slowly chew the chocolate and become as fully aware of its taste and texture as possible. This will help you to feel more satisfied with one portion.

Only a couple of comments, then, are really necessary before you begin cooking. One is that baking chocolate easily burns—and then tastes terrible. It's really important, therefore, that you keep a steady eye on the chocolate as you cook and melt it.

Also, many of the recipes for chocolate call for "cream of tartar." Please don't try and skip this ingredient, because it's necessary for eliminating the bitter taste of unsweetened baking chocolate. Cream of tartar is inexpensive and readily available in the spice section of any grocery store.

In preparing these recipes, I've made every attempt to keep the ingredients as healthy for you as possible. Almost every recipe uses egg substitute and unsaturated or monosaturated oils to keep the cholesterol count down. I have also kept the sodium count down as low as possible. And finally, I've used whole wheat flour in the baking recipes.

Desserts Sweetened with Nutrasweet Brand Sweetener (Aspartame)

Nutrasweet brand sweetener is made of two amino acids, phenylalanine and aspartic acid. It tastes good, with little aftertaste, but it loses its sweetness when heated or stored for a long time.

The amino acid phenylalanine, while otherwise safe, has raised some concern because of its ability to block the production of serotonin in the brain. Some people report that when they consume too much aspartame, they feel jittery, depressed, or confused, and this is believed to be related to the lower serotonin levels which can accompany the ingestion of phenylalanine.

The FDA approved aspartame in 1981 and there is no evidence presently that it will be recalled. Other sugar alternatives will be on the market soon, including one called "Sunette" (Acesulfame K), a sweetener said to be 200 times sweeter than sugar and heat stable. However, at least one prominent scientist has called for more tests on Sunette because of some data linking Sunette to breast and lung cancer in animals.

My review of the literature on aspartame makes me feel that when used in moderation, the product is safe. I have concerns based on several studies about pregnant women using it, however, and I know that if I were carrying a child right now, I'd avoid aspartame during the pregnancy just to be on the safe side.

The recipes with Nutrasweet brand sweetener call for adding the sweetener *after* the heating process is completed. This is one important step you can take to enjoy aspartame without worry.

CHOCOLATE NONFAT FROZEN YOGURT
Serves 1
(215 calories and 1.25 grams fat)

    ½ cup plain nonfat yogurt
    16 Equal packets
    2 teaspoons unsweetened cocoa powder
    1 cup nonfat milk

In a deep bowl, beat the yogurt with an electric mixer for 2 minutes on low speed, until it is very frothy. Put in the freezer for 45 minutes, or until ice crystals start to form on the top and bottom of the yogurt. Blend in the remaining ingredients with an eggbeater on low speed, and freeze an additional hour (or until the mixture hardens throughout). Blend with an eggbeater again at low speed until the mixture is the texture of soft ice cream. Delicious!

Variations: Add ¹⁄₁₆ teaspoon (approximately 2 drops) of sugar-free flavoring such as peppermint, cherry, or almond extract to make Chocolate-Mint, Cherry-Chocolate, Chocolate-Amaretto Frozen Yogurt.

MILK CHOCOLATE CANDY BAR
Serves 1
(146 calories and 8 grams of fat)

2 teaspoons nonfat milk
¹⁄₁₆ teaspoon (approximately 2 pinchs) cream
   of tartar
7 Equal packets
1 teaspoon powdered nonfat milk
½ ounce (one square) unsweetened baking
   chocolate
1 teaspoon low-calorie margarine

This recipe calls for three small microwaveproof bowls and a sheet of wax paper.

In the first bowl, heat the nonfat milk in the microwave oven on high for 20 seconds, or until warm. Stir in the cream of tartar, Equal, and powdered milk. Stir well.

In the second bowl, heat the chocolate in the microwave oven on high for 2 minutes. Put the margarine in the third bowl. When the chocolate has cooked for 2 minutes, put the margarine in the microwave oven so that both bowls are side by side. Cook both simultaneously for 1 minute.

Pour the margarine over the chocolate and stir while the chocolate melts completely. Stir in the milk mixture and blend for about 2 minutes, until the candy thickens and cools.

Pour the candy onto the wax paper and, using a dull knife and the back of a large spoon, shape it into a candy bar, about 10-by-2-inches. Freeze for approximately a half hour. Irresistible!

MILK CHOCOLATE
FREEZER FUDGE
Serves 1
(175 calories and 10 grams of fat)

1 tablespoon nonfat milk
1 tablespoon powdered nonfat milk
$\frac{1}{16}$ teaspoon (approximately 2 pinches) cream
   of tartar
7 Equal packets
1 square ($\frac{1}{2}$ ounce) unsweetened baking
   chocolate
1 teaspoon low-calorie margarine
2 tablespoons crumbled rice cake

This recipe calls for three small microwaveproof bowls
and a sheet of wax paper.

In the first bowl, heat the milk in the microwave oven on
high for 20 seconds. Add the milk, cream of tartar, and Equal.

In the second bowl, heat the chocolate on high for 2
minutes. Put the margarine in the third bowl and place next to
the chocolate in the microwave oven. Heat both for 1 minute
on high.

Pour the margarine over the chocolate and stir until the
chocolate melts. Add the milk mixture and blend until the
fudge starts to cool and thicken. Add in the crumbled rice
cake and blend thoroughly. Spoon onto the wax paper and
freeze for 2 hours. This delicious fudge stays chewy, and has
the taste and consistency of fattening fudge.

CHOCOLATE CHIP MILK SHAKE
Serves 1 generously
(210.5 calories and 8 grams of fat)

½ ounce (1 square) unsweetened baking
 chocolate
8 Equal packets
1 capful (⅛ teaspoon) sugar-free vanilla extract
⅛ teaspoon cream of tartar
1 cup nonfat milk
2 cups ice, crushed or small cubes

Put the ingredients in a blender in the order listed and blend on high speed for 1 minute, or until the ice is finely chopped.

Variations: Mint Chocolate Chip Milk Shake: Add ¹⁄₁₆ teaspoon pure peppermint extract. One drop of green food coloring can also be added to achieve the traditional color of mint chocolate chip ice cream.

Chocolate Chocolate Chip Milk Shake: Add 1 tablespoon cocoa powder to the mixture. This increases the calorie and fat count to 232 calories and 9 grams of fat.

SUGAR-FREE CREAMY MILK CHOCOLATE HOT COCOA
Serves 1
(124 calories and 1 gram of fat)

1 cup nonfat milk
1 tablespoon unsweetened cocoa powder
4 Equal packets

In the microwave oven, heat the milk on high for 2½ minutes. Stir in the cocoa and Equal until dissolved. Delicious and filling for evening "hungries."

LOW-CALORIE HOT COCOA
Serves 1
(70 calories and 1 gram of fat)

1 cup water
2 tablespoons powdered nonfat milk
1 tablespoon unsweetened cocoa powder
4 Equal packets

In the microwave oven, heat the water on high for 2 minutes. Stir in the milk powder until dissolved, then add the cocoa powder and blend with a spoon. Add the Equal last and stir. Delicious and contains no tropical oils—less expensive than packaged sugar-free cocoa mixes, too!

SUGAR-FREE
MOCHA CAFÉ AU LAIT
Serves 1
(45 calories and .5 grams of fat)

1 cup prepared hot coffee (can be brewed,
    instant, or decaffeinated)
2 teaspoons unsweetened cocoa powder
1 tablespoon powdered nonfat milk
3 Equal packets

Add the cocoa, milk powder, and Equal to the hot coffee and pour into a blender. Blend on high speed for 1 minute, or until the mixture begins foaming. Pour into a large coffee mug (to make room for the foamy top) and microwave for 30 seconds on high.

Variations: Add 1 drop peppermint, cherry, or almond extract.

TROPICAL CHOCOLATE FREEZER CANDY

Serves 1
(72 calories and 1 gram of fat)

½ large very ripe banana
1 teaspoon unsweetened cocoa powder
3 Equal packets

Mix the ingredients with an electric mixer on low speed for 1 minute, until smooth. Spread on wax paper and freeze for a half hour.

CRISPY-RICE CHOCOLATE CANDY

Serves 1
(183 calories and 10 grams of fat)

½ ounce (1 square) unsweetened baking
    chocolate
½ teaspoon canola, safflower, or sunflower
    cooking oil
1 teaspoon powdered nonfat milk
1/16 teaspoon (approximately 2 pinches) cream
    of tartar
6 Equal packets
3 tablespoons uncooked white rice

In a shallow microwaveproof bowl, melt the chocolate with the cooking oil in the microwave oven on high for 2 minutes. Stir in the powdered milk, cream of tartar, and Equal until thoroughly blended. Before the mixture can cool, stir in the rice and mix until all the rice is coated with chocolate.

Spoon the mixture onto wax paper and flatten to about ¼-inch high. Freeze for a half hour before eating.

CHOCOLATE-MALT MOUSSE
Serves 1
(90 calories and 7 grams of fat)

⅛ cup powdered nonfat milk
½ tablespoon canola, safflower, or sunflower
    cooking oil
2 tablespoons cold water
4 Equal packets
¼ teaspoon unsweetened cocoa powder

In a deep bowl, blend the ingredients in the order listed with a large spoon. Mix thoroughly with an electric mixer on slow or medium speed until the mousse is blended and whipped.

CREAMY DOUBLE-CHOCOLATE FUDGE
Serves 1
(151 calories and 8 grams of fat)

4½ teaspoons *skim* evaporated milk
½ ounce (1 square) unsweetened baking
    chocolate
10 Equal packets
¹⁄₁₆ teaspoon (approximately 2 pinches) cream
    of tartar

In a saucepan, cook the evaporated milk over low heat. Stir continuously until small bubbles form around the edges. Break the chocolate square as much as possible and place in the milk. Still on low heat, push the chocolate with a spoon until it just begins to melt. Remove the pan from the heat and continue to push the chocolate with the spoon. If the chocolate stops melting, briefly (30 seconds at most) return the pan to the low heat. When the chocolate is completely melted and the milk is absorbed, continue stirring the mixture for 1 minute.

Blend in the Equal and cream of tartar by creaming them together with the back of a large spoon. Spoon onto wax paper and refrigerate for 15 minutes. Absolutely delicious!

FROSTED FUDGE ALMONDS
Serves 1
(180 calories and 10 grams of fat)

½ ounce (1 square) unsweetened baking
    chocolate
7 Equal packets
1/16 teaspoon (approximately 2 pinches) cream
    of tartar
2 teaspoons *skim* evaporated milk
7 unsalted dry roasted almonds

Cook the chocolate in a medium-size microwaveproof
bowl in the microwave oven for 2 minutes on high. Stir to set
the melting process into motion by creaming with the back of
a large spoon until the chocolate stops melting. If still not
entirely melted, microwave on high for an additional 45 seconds.

Stir in 6 Equal packets and the cream of tartar until
blended and then add the evaporated milk. The mixture will cool
and begin to harden, but continue stirring until the milk is dis-
tributed throughout. With your fingers, form the mixture into 7
balls, approximately ½-inch in diameter. Press 1 almond into
each ball and sprinkle the 1 remaining Equal packet over the
7 balls. Refrigerate for at least 15 minutes before eating.

PERFECT FUDGE FROSTING
Serves 1
(89 calories and 6 grams of fat)

1 tablespoon soft low-calorie margarine
8 Equal packets
¼ teaspoon sugar-free vanilla extract
1 teaspoon unsweetened cocoa powder
1/16 teaspoon (approximately 2 pinches) cream
    of tartar

Place the margarine in a bowl. Blend the next four
ingredients, one at a time, into the margarine using the back
of a large spoon.

Serving suggestion: Top a plain rice cake with one third of the frosting for a delicious 65-calorie, 2-fat-gram treat!

LOW-CALORIE CHOCOLATE MUNCHIES
Serves 1
(81 calories and less than 1 gram of fat)

1 cup plain air-popped popcorn
1 teaspoon unsweetened cocoa powder
5 Equal packets

Put the popcorn in deep bowl. Mix the cocoa and Equal together in a small bowl, and pour over the popcorn. Stir until all the kernels are dusted brown.

PEANUT BUTTER CUP CRUNCHIES
Serves 1
(150 calories and 7 grams of fat)

1 tablespoon peanut butter
9 Equal packets
1 teaspoon unsweetened cocoa powder
½ cup plain air-popped popcorn
    (approximately 20 popped kernels)

In a bowl, mix the peanut butter completely with 4 Equal packets. In a separate shallow bowl, mix the cocoa powder with the remaining 5 Equal packets.

With your fingers, roll each kernel of popcorn in the peanut butter mixture until about three-quarters covered, then roll in the cocoa mix until completely dusted. Delicious!

CHOCOLATE DREAM PUDDING
Serves 1
(132 calories and 2 grams of fat)

½ cup rolling boiling water
1 envelope (.25 ounce) plain gelatin powder
½ cup cold water
3 tablespoons *skim* evaporated milk
7 Equal packets
¼ cup powdered nonfat milk
1 tablespoon unsweetened cocoa powder

In a deep bowl, mix the hot water and gelatin with an electric mixer on medium speed for 1 minute. Add the cold water and beat an additional 1 minute. Add the evaporated milk and beat on medium speed until the mixture is frothy. Refrigerate for 45 minutes.

Remove from the refrigerator and add the Equal, nonfat milk powder, and cocoa. Beat on medium speed for 2 minutes, until the entire mixture attains the consistency of pudding.

Serving suggestion: Fold in 1 cup of sugar-free, drained fruit salad for a tasty 234-calorie side dish.

For Chocolate-Covered
Fruits and Nuts

CHOCOLATE DIP AND DRIZZLE
Serves 1
(121 calories and 8 grams of fat)

½ ounce (1 square) unsweetened baking
    chocolate
1/16 teaspoon (approximately 2 pinches) cream
    of tartar
7 Equal packets

In a small microwaveproof bowl, melt the chocolate in the microwave oven on high for 1 minute and 45 seconds.

With a small spoon, stir the chocolate to begin the melting process, and break the chocolate—using the side of the spoon like a knife—into seven to ten smaller pieces.

Put back into the microwave oven on high for 1½ minutes. Stir in the cream of tartar and Equal until all are blended.

DIPPING SUGGESTIONS:

> 1 cup strawberries (45 calories, 0 grams fat)
> 1 medium orange, peeled and sectioned (65 calories, 0 grams fat)
> 10 cherries (50 calories, 0 grams fat)
> 1 medium kiwi fruit, peeled and sliced (45 calories, 0 grams fat)

To dip: Wash and thoroughly dry the fruit to be dipped and have it ready so that the chocolate doesn't have a chance to cool off. Hand-dip the fruit one at a time, covering about half of the item. Cool on wax paper and place in the refrigerator until the chocolate hardens (about 5 minutes).

DRIZZLING SUGGESTIONS:

> 1 cup plain air-popped popcorn (55 calories, 0 grams fat)
> 10 dry-roasted almonds (75 calories, 7 grams fat)
> 2 rice cakes (70 calories, 0 grams fat)

To drizzle: Place items to be drizzled on wax paper with about 2 inches between the items. Using a large spoon to control the flow, slowly pour (drizzle) the chocolate over the items. Avoid touching the chocolate after it has been poured—by allowing the chocolate to harden after pouring, an attractive gloss will develop.

NUTTY CHOCOLATE BAR
Serves 1
(180 calories and 10 grams of fat)

1 tablespoon peanut butter
½ ounce (1 square) unsweetened baking
   chocolate
12 Equal packets
1/16 teaspoon (approximately 2 pinches) cream
   of tartar

Place the peanut butter in the middle of a saucepan, and put the chocolate on top of the peanut butter. Stir constantly over low heat until about one third of the chocolate is melted. Remove the saucepan from the heat and continue stirring until the mixture is blended. Let cool for 1 minute without stirring, then add the Equal and cream of tartar, and blend completely.

Spoon the mixture onto wax paper and form into a candy bar, using the back of a spoon and a knife to help form a bar approximately 6-by-1-inch. Freeze for 15 minutes to harden before eating.

RICH BUTTER-CREAM
FUDGE CANDY
Serves 1
(85 calories and 6 grams of fat)

1 tablespoon low-calorie margarine
1 teaspoon unsweetened cocoa powder
¼ teaspoon sugar-free vanilla extract
1 teaspoon *skim* evaporated milk
6 Equal packets

Melt the margarine in a saucepan over low heat, stirring constantly. When the margarine is completely melted, remove the pan from the heat and add the cocoa, vanilla, and evaporated milk, and stir. Pour into a bowl and allow to cool for 5 minutes before adding the Equal. Spread in a thin layer on wax paper and refrigerate until the candy is hard. Extremely rich!

CANDIED COCOA POPCORN
Serves 1
(140 calories and 6 grams of fat)

1 cup plain air-popped popcorn
Rich Butter-Cream Fudge Candy (see page
   136)

Make the Rich Butter-Cream Fudge Candy according to
the directions, but instead of refrigerating the mixture, pour it
over the popcorn for a delicious treat.

CHOCOLATE MILK SHAKE
Serves 1
(125 calories and 1 gram of fat)

1 cup nonfat milk
1 cup ice, crushed or small ice cubes
1 tablespoon unsweetened cocoa powder
4 Equal packets

Put all the ingredients in a blender and mix at low speed
for 1 minute.

Variations: Add 1 capful of sugar-free flavoring extract,
such as cherry, peppermint, or almond.

"BRANDY" ALEXANDER
Serves 1
(215 calories and 1.5 grams of fat)

1 cup nonfat milk
1 cup ice, crushed or small ice cubes
2 tablespoons unsweetened cocoa powder
5 Equal packets
⅛ cup (1 ounce or 2 tablespoons) 80-proof
   light rum

Put all the ingredients in a blender and mix at low speed
for 1 to 1½ minutes.

Variations: The rum may be replaced with any other 80-proof liquor, such as vodka, whiskey, or gin, and the calorie and fat count will remain the same. Do not use brandy, cordials, or liqueurs, however, as they contain sugars and more calories.

CHOCOLATE SODA FLOAT
Serves 1 or 2
(One large serving equals 67 calories and less than 1 gram of fat; two servings equal 33 calories and less than 1 gram of fat)

    1 cup diet cream soda pop
    ½ cup nonfat milk
    1 tablespoon unsweetened cocoa powder
    1 cup ice, crushed or small cubes

Put all the ingredients into a blender and blend at medium speed for 1 to 2 minutes.

Variations: Substitute the cream soda with diet root beer or cola.

Desserts Sweetened with Honey

Honey is a sweetener with a different, yet enjoyable, flavor. Because it is easily digested and doesn't send the blood sugar levels soaring, it's safe for Chocolate Bingers to use. One thing to keep in mind with honey, though, is that despite the fact it's a natural sweetener it still is fairly high in calories. Be sure and stick to the recipe measurements when cooking with honey so that your calorie counts stay in line with The Dream Diet.

Carob powder is another ingredient used in the recipes that follow. Although carob wouldn't fool even the most relaxed chocoholic, it can satisfy a craving for chocolate. I like carob because it's low in fat and the finely ground powder makes for a smooth texture in cooking. Be sure, when you purchase carob powder, to get only the unsweetened variety, usually labeled "pure carob powder." You can purchase this in most grocery stores or health food stores.

CAROB-HONEY TAFFY
Serves 1
(48 calories and less than 1 gram of fat)

1½ teaspoons honey
1 teaspoon unsweetened pure carob powder
1 teaspoon unsweetened cocoa powder
½ teaspoon powdered nonfat milk

Put the honey in a bowl and blend the other ingredients in, one at a time. Spread the mixture onto wax paper and freeze at least 1 hour before eating. Peel off wax paper like taffy and tastes delicious! Low in calories, too.

CAROB SYRUP
Serves 1
(84 calories and less than 1 gram of fat)

1 tablespoon honey
1 teaspoon unsweetened pure carob powder
2 teaspoons unsweetened cocoa powder
1 tablespoon very hot water

Put the honey in a bowl and blend in the carob and cocoa completely. Add the hot water and stir until the mixture becomes runny. This syrup can be refrigerated and it will stay a good consistency for pouring on bisquits, bagels, toast, and rice cakes.

DEVIL'S FOOD CAKE
Serves 1
(250 calories and 6 grams of fat)

1 large egg
1 tablespoon unsweetened pure carob powder
1 tablespoon unsweetened cocoa powder
¼ teaspoon baking powder
2 tablespoons honey
2 teaspoons *skim* evaporated milk

Mix all the ingredients thoroughly in a shallow microwaveproof baking dish. Cook in the microwave oven on high for 3 minutes. Easy to make and tastes delicious!

MILK CHOCOLATE CREPE
Serves 1
(244 calories and 7 grams of fat)

1 large egg
1 tablespoon unsweetened cocoa powder
½ teaspoon low-calorie margarine
2 tablespoons honey
1 tablespoon *skim* evaporated milk
¼ teaspoon baking powder
¼ teaspoon sugar-free vanilla extract

Mix all the ingredients completely in a shallow microwaveproof baking dish. Cook in the microwave oven on high for 3 minutes. The crepe stays thin and has a texture like sponge cake.

CHOCOLATE HEALTH BAR
Serves 1
(102 calories and 8 grams of fat)

½ ounce (1 square) unsweetened baking
  chocolate
1 tablespoon unsweetened pure carob powder
1 tablespoon honey

In a microwaveproof bowl, melt the chocolate in the microwave oven on high for 2 minutes. Stir until completely melted. Add the carob and honey, and stir thoroughly. Spoon the mixture into a big ball and place on wax paper. With the back of a large spoon, press down on the ball until flattened. Shape into a rectangle, like a candy bar, and freeze for 1 hour before eating.

CHOCOLATE MACAROONS
Serves 1
(200 calories and 8 grams of fat)

¼ cup unsweetened shredded coconut
1 tablespoon cocoa powder
1½ tablespoons honey

Put the coconut in a bowl and mix in the cocoa powder. Add 1 tablespoon of the honey and blend, then add the remaining honey and mix thoroughly, using the back of the spoon if necessary. Form into balls on wax paper and freeze for a half hour, or until firm, before eating.

COCONUT-CHOCOLATE CANDY
Serves 1
(177 calories and 10 grams of fat)

½ ounce (1 square) unsweetened baking
   chocolate
2 teaspoons honey
¹⁄₁₆ teaspoon (approximately 2 pinches) cream
   of tartar
2 tablespoons unsweetened shredded coconut

In a microwaveproof bowl, melt the chocolate in the microwave oven on high for 2 minutes. Stir the chocolate briefly to continue the melting process. Next, add the honey and stir (it will melt into the chocolate). Add the cream of tartar and blend in thoroughly. Stir in the coconut until it is completely covered with the chocolate mix.

Spoon onto wax paper and flatten into a candy bar shape. Freeze for a half hour, or until firm, before eating. Absolutely delicious!

Desserts Sweetened with Fructose

Fructose is my favorite sweetener, and one which I highly recommend for all chocoholics, but especially Chocolate Bingers. Made from the sugar of fruits, fructose tastes almost identical to refined sugar, but without the associated problems that go along with other sweeteners.

The benefits of using fructose include:

- Knowing that your blood sugar level will stay stable when you eat foods prepared with it. This will eliminate the anxiety and mood swings that accompany eating foods prepared with refined sugar.
- Knowing that fructose isn't made of harmful chemicals.

- Knowing that fructose will allow you to have your chocolate cake and eat it, too. With fructose, you'll be able to eat chocolate treats which taste almost identical to the sugary snacks you may have binged on in the past. Only now you won't feel anxiously compelled to go on an all-out eating binge!

Fructose can be purchased in bulk powder form at most health food stores, or in packets with individual servings. I prefer to buy it in bulk when I bake with it.

One thing to keep in mind about fructose, though: It has just about the same number of calories as sugar. So, while it's not exactly a "diet" sweetener, it will help you on your diet by helping you to cut down on the *amount* of food you eat.

DELICIOUS HOME-STYLE CHOCOLATE CHIP COOKIES
Makes 15 cookies
(97 calories and 3 grams of fat each)

    1 batch Chocolate Chips (recipe follows)
    ⅓ cup low-calorie margarine
    ¾ cup granulated fructose
    ¼ cup egg substitute
    ½ teaspoon sugar-free vanilla extract
    ¾ cup whole wheat flour
    ¼ teaspoon baking powder

Make the Chocolate Chips before preparing the cookie dough. Preheat the oven to 375°F and spray a cookie sheet with nonstick cooking spray (such as Pam) no-stick cooking spray.

In a bowl, blend the margarine, fructose, egg substitute, and vanilla together thoroughly. Add the flour and baking powder, and stir until the batter is completely mixed. Carefully fold in the Chocolate Chips and spoon onto the cookie sheet to make 15 cookies. Bake for 7 to 9 minutes.

Variation: Chocolate Chocolate Chip Cookies: (Each cookie has 100 calories and 3 grams of fat.) Follow the chocolate chip cookie recipe, as outlined above. After mixing in the flour and baking powder, add 2 tablespoons of unsweetened cocoa powder to the batter and blend thoroughly. Fold in the Chocolate Chips and bake as directed.

Chocolate Chips
Makes enough for 15 cookies
**(16.3 calories and 1 gram of fat per portion
[¹⁄₁₅ of a batch], the calories and fat have already been
included in the chocolate chip cookie recipes, above)**

½ ounce (1 square) unsweetened baking
 chocolate
1 tablespoon low-calorie margarine
2 tablespoons granulated fructose
¹⁄₁₆ teaspoon (approximately 2 pinches) cream
 of tartar

In a microwaveproof bowl, cook the chocolate and margarine together in the microwave oven for 1½ minutes on high. Stir together to complete the melting process for the chocolate. Add the fructose and cream of tartar, and mix thoroughly.

Allow the mixture to cool for 2 minutes and then spoon the mixture onto a large sheet of wax paper, making tiny "chip-size" drops about ¼-to-⅓-inch in diameter. Put the wax paper and chips in the freezer. Allow the chips to freeze until completely solid, about 30 to 45 minutes. The chips can then be used like regular chocolate chips, and will fold into cookie batter easily.

MOIST AND CHEWY BROWNIES
Makes 16 brownies
(52 calories and 2 grams of fat each)

½ ounce (1 square) unsweetened baking
chocolate

¼ cup low-calorie margarine

⅛ teaspoon cream of tartar

¼ cup egg substitute

½ cup granulated fructose

1 teaspoon sugar-free vanilla extract

¼ cup whole wheat flour

Preheat the oven to 350°F and spray nonstick cooking spray (such as Pam) on the bottom and sides of an 8-by-8-inch baking pan.

Melt the chocolate and margarine together in a large microwaveproof bowl in the microwave oven for 1½ minutes on high. Stir until the chocolate is completely melted and mixed with the margarine.

Stir in the remaining ingredients, one by one, until the batter is completely blended. Pour the batter into the cooking pan and bake for 20 to 22 minutes. The brownies are done when the center springs to the touch, or when a fork pierced through the middle is clean when removed from the brownies. Cool completely, then cut into 16 brownies, 2-by-2-inches each.

DOUBLE-CHOCOLATE FROSTED CAKE

Makes 16 pieces, approximately 2-by-2-inches each
(72 calories and 1.6 grams of fat each)

- ½ ounce (1 square) unsweetened baking chocolate
- 1 teaspoon low-calorie margarine
- ¼ teaspoon sugar-free vanilla extract
- ⅛ teaspoon cream of tartar
- ½ cup granulated fructose
- ¾ cup nonfat milk
- 1 tablespoon honey
- 2 tablespoons unsweetened cocoa powder
- ⅔ cup whole wheat flour
- 1 teaspoon baking powder
- ¼ cup egg substitute
- 1 batch Chocolate Frosting (recipe follows)

Preheat the oven to 350°F. Spray nonstick cooking spray (such as Pam) on the bottom and sides of an 8-by-8-inch baking pan.

Put the chocolate, margarine, vanilla extract, and cream of tartar into a large microwaveproof bowl and cook in the microwave oven on high for 1½ minutes. Stir until the chocolate is completely melted and the ingredients are blended.

Stir in the remaining ingredients, one at a time, until the batter is completely blended. Pour the batter into the baking pan and bake for 20 minutes. After baking, allow the cake to cool in the baking pan for 30 minutes before frosting it with the Chocolate Frosting.

CHOCOLATE FROSTING
Makes enough for 1 Double-Chocolate Frosted Cake
(17 calories and 0.8 gram of fat per portion
[$1/16$ of a batch], the calorie and fat counts
in this frosting are already included in the
Double-Chocolate Frosted Cake recipe, above)

2 tablespoons low-calorie margarine, softened
1 tablespoon unsweetened cocoa powder
3 tablespoons granulated fructose

Combine all ingredients and spread on cake.

QUICK CAROB SNACK
Serves 1
(210 calories and less than 1 gram of fat)

2 tablespoons unsweetened pure carob powder
1 tablespoon granulated fructose
1 banana

Mix the carob powder and fructose together in a bowl. Peel the banana and dip it into the powder mix until it is completely covered, and eat.

Desserts Sweetened with Corn Syrup

Corn syrup is mildly sweet with an extremely appealing flavor. It helps give a nice texture to baked goods, and I think you'll find, as I do, that it's enjoyable to use in baking.

DEVIL'S FOOD COOKIES
Makes 12 cookies
(75 calories and less than 1 gram of fat each)

2 tablespoons unsweetened cocoa powder
½ cup light corn syrup
2 tablespoons (⅛ cup) egg substitute
3 tablespoons nonfat milk
¼ teaspoon baking powder
1 tablespoon honey
¾ cup whole wheat flour

Preheat the oven to 325°F and spray nonstick cooking spray (such as Pam) on a cookie sheet.

Blend the cocoa powder, corn syrup, egg substitute, and milk together in a large bowl. Stir in the baking powder and honey. Add the flour and blend completely.

Spoon the dough onto the cookie sheet to make 12 cookies. Bake for 5 to 7 minutes.

CHEWY ROLL CANDY
Serves 1
(212.5 calories and 8 grams of fat)

½ ounce (1 square) unsweetened baking
    chocolate
2 tablespoons light corn syrup
¹⁄₁₆ teaspoon (approximately 2 pinches) cream
    of tartar

In a microwaveproof bowl, heat the chocolate in the microwave oven for 2 minutes on high. Add the corn syrup and cream of tartar. Cook in the microwave oven for 1 minute on high—the mixture will bubble as it cooks.

Pour the mixture onto wax paper and freeze for 3 to 5 minutes, or until the candy becomes chewy. Do not overfreeze, as the candy will become too hard to eat and will lose its appealing chewy taste.

CHOCOLATE PUDDING BREAD
Serves 8
(182 calories and 3 grams of fat each)

½ cup egg substitute
2 tablespoons unsweetened cocoa powder
¾ cup light corn syrup
1 cup nonfat milk
1 cup whole wheat flour
1 teaspoon baking powder
3 tablespoons low-calorie margarine

Put the egg substitute, cocoa powder, corn syrup, and milk into a medium-size pot and heat over low heat. Stir constantly with a wire whisk until the mixture starts to boil with small bubbles (about 5 to 7 minutes). Remove from the heat and continue to stir 1 minute.

Preheat the oven to 350°F and spray an 8-by-8-inch baking pan with nonstick spray (such as Pam).

Using an electric mixer blend the mixture at medium speed for 2 minutes. Add the flour and baking powder and stir with a spoon until completely blended. Bake for 25 minutes. Remove from the oven and spread the margarine over the top of the bread; the margarine will melt as it is spread. Cut into eight pieces and serve hot or refrigerated.

11

Ready-Made Chocolate Snacks and Drinks

Your daily chocolate snack doesn't have to be home-made. You may feel free to eat a chocolate treat from the store, if you choose, given that it meets three guidelines:

1. The calorie and fat counts in the product are listed. Never eat any chocolate if you can't verify how many calories or grams of fat are in it.
2. The product does not have refined sugar in it. This is especially important for Chocolate Bingers. Many so-called "dietetic" or low-calorie choco-late snacks available in stores have refined sugar in them. Sometimes this means straining your eyes over the fine print on the ingredients list, but it's worth it to avoid an eating binge.
3. The product does not contain "tropical oils"—palm kernel, palm, or hydrogenated coconut oil. These oils are more highly saturated in fat than beef! While I'm not a fanatic who would worry about having a tropical oil occasionally show up in a meal, I think it's really important that we take the time to avoid these oils as much as possible.

Besides being very fattening, they are major causes of high serum cholesterol levels. What's especially surprising, even maddening, to me is how many sugar-free chocolate and carob snacks sold in "health food stores" contain these tropical oils. It really is a case of buyer beware!

Some of the snacks listed, such as the candy bars, fit into The Chocoholic's Dream Diet only if they are split into smaller portions. Obviously, it would be impossible to ask a Chocolate Binger, and many other chocoholics, to eat just three fourths of a candy bar and stop at that. I've included these directions, though, because *some* chocoholics, who binge only out of lack of understanding and information about the calorie/fat content of chocolate, *will* be able to eat a part of a candy bar and be satisfied.

I think it's important for all chocoholics to be aware of how high in calories and fat many of the "dietetic" chocolate treats are. I remember how I used to scan the "diet" section of the grocery store, hoping to find something chocolaty and delicious that wouldn't put the weight on me.

More than once, I bought a sugar-free chocolate bar thinking that the term "sugar-free" implied "calorie-free." I bought the bar, paying attention only to the little slogan written on its side that promised "only 22 calories per serving." I'd happily eat the entire chocolate bar, feeling relieved that I was able to eat something so closely resembling the real thing without having to pay the price in calories.

Imagine my shock when, after eating the entire bar, I read the candy wrapper more closely and found that the whole candy bar contained 420 calories and 35 grams of fat! I would have saved half those calories and fats, and probably been much more satisfied, by having a plain old Hershey's bar!

The point of this story is to caution you about the ambiguous meaning of the word "dietetic." In grocery stores, the term most often means foods especially prepared for people on low-salt diets and diabetic individuals who cannot tolerate refined sugar for health reasons. Dietetic means "special diet," not "low calorie."

Much of what is listed here is designed to increase your awareness, and is not necessarily a recommendation that you should eat every type of chocolate snack listed. Many of the foods in this chapter are high in tropical oils or contain suspect artificial sweeteners. Use this chapter as a guide to knowing which chocolate treats are just that—treats—and not tricks.

Frozen Chocolate Confections, Sugar Free

Crystal Light "Cool 'n Creamy" Double Fudge Bars
  One 1.8-fluidounce bar, 50 calories, 2 grams fat
  Note: Made with corn syrup and hydrogenated coconut and palm kernel oils.

Crystal Light "Cool 'n Creamy" Chocolate
    Covered Vanilla Ice Milk Bars
  One 1.8-fluidounce bar, 50 calories, 2 grams fat
  Note: Made with corn syrup and hydrogenated coconut and palm kernel oils.

Dreyer's Diabetic Ice Cream, Chocolate
  4 ounces, 140 calories, 7 grams fat
  Note: Made with fructose and sorbitol.

Eskimo Pie Sandwiches, Sugar Free, Chocolate
Wafers, Vanilla Frozen Dairy Dessert
One 3.2-fluidounce sandwich, 150 calories, 6 grams
fat
Note: Made with NutraSweet and sorbitol.

Fudgsicle Sugar-Free Fudge Pops
One 1.75-fluidounce bar, 35 calories, 1 gram fat
Note: Made with NutraSweet.

Knudsen Chocolate Diabetic Ice Cream
½ cup, 120 calories, 7 grams fat
Note: Made with sorbitol.

Skinny Dip Premium Low Calorie Frozen
Dessert, Chocolate Flavored
4 ounces, 36 calories, 0 grams fat
Note: Made with fructose. Available at selected ice-
cream and frozen-yogurt shops nationwide.

Sweet 'n Low Dietary Bars, "Vanilla Artificially Flavored
Bars With Premium Chocolate Flavored Coating"
One 2.50-fluidounce bar, 120 calories, 8 grams fat
Note: Made with coconut and soybean oils, mannitol,
chocolate liqueur, and crystalline fructose.

TCBY (The Country's Best Yogurt)
29–35 calories per fluidounce, depending on flavor,
less than 1 gram fat per ounce
Note: This product is sweetened with fruit juice. Not
available for purchase outside of yogurt shops.

Weight Watchers Chocolate Mousse Bars
One 1.75-fluidounce bar, 45 calories, less than 1
gram fat
Note: Made with NutraSweet and sorbitol.

Frozen Chocolate Confections
Made with Sugar

Breyers Chocolate-Chocolate Chip All Natural Ice Cream
½ cup, 180 calories, 3 grams fat
Note: Made with sugar.

Carnation Smooth 'n Lite 96% Fat Free
Ice Milk, Chocolate Flavor
1 cup, 200 calories, 6 grams fat
Note: Made with sugar and corn syrup.

Dreyers All Natural Frozen Yogurt Inspirations, Chocolate
½ cup, 110 calories, 1.5 grams fat
Note: Made with sugar and corn syrup.

Dreyers Grand Light, Light Dairy Dessert, Marble Fudge
1 cup, 240 calories, 8 grams fat
Note: Made with sugar and corn syrup.

Dreyers Grand Light, Light Dairy Dessert, Mocha Fudge
1 cup, 220 calories, 8 grams fat
Note: Made with sugar and corn syrup.

Dreyers Grand Light, Light Dairy Dessert, Rocky Road
¾ cup, 195 calories, 7.5 grams fat
Note: Made with sugar and corn syrup.

Eskimo Pie, Dark Chocolate Coating, Vanilla Ice Cream
One 3-ounce bar, 180 calories, 12 grams fat
Note: To bring this into the calorie/fat range, you may
eat ¾ bar for 135 calories and 9 grams of fat. Made
with sugar and coconut oil.

Haagen-Dazs Chocolate Ice Cream
¼ cup, 135 calories, 8.5 grams fat
Note: Made with sugar and corn syrup.

Haagen-Dazs Chocolate-Chocolate Chip Ice Cream
¼ cup, 145 calories, 9 grams fat
Note: Made with sugar and chocolate liqueur.

Haagen-Dazs Deep Chocolate Ice Cream
¼ cup, 145 calories, 7 grams fat
Note: Made with sugar.

Haagen-Dazs Deep Chocolate Peanut Butter Ice Cream
⅛ cup plus 1 tablespoon (1½ ounces), 125 calories,
7 grams fat
Note: Please note the small serving size in order to fit
into the calorie/fat range. Made with sugar.

Haagen-Dazs Gourmet Frozen Yogurt, Chocolate Flavor
¾ cup (6 ounces), 180 calories, 6 grams fat
Note: Sold only in Haagen-Dazs Shoppes, located
around the nation. Made with sugar.

Jell-O Pudding Pops Frozen Pudding Snack on a Stick,
Chocolate or Chocolate-Vanilla Swirl Flavors
One 1.75-ounce bar, 80 calories, 2 grams fat
Note: Made with sugar and tropical oils.

Knudsen Nice N' Light Chocolate Ice Milk
1 cup, 200 calories, 4 grams fat
Note: Made with sugar and corn syrup.

Knudsen Nice N' Light Chocolate Chip Ice Milk
1 cup, 220 calories, 6 grams fat
Note: Made with sugar, corn syrup, and partially hydrogenated coconut oil.

Knudsen Nice N' Light Chocolate Brownie Nut or Chocolate Marble or Rocky Road Flavored Ice Milk
1 cup, 240 calories, 6 grams fat
Note: Made with sugar and corn syrup. The chocolate-
brownie-nut flavor is made with partially hydrogenated coconut oil.

Loft's "Tofulite" Chocolate Bars
  One 3.2-ounce bar, 240 calories, 15 grams fat
  Note: To bring this into the calorie/fat range, you may
    eat ½ bar for 120 calories and 7.5 grams of fat.
    Made with sugar and corn syrup.

Mocha Mix Non-Dairy Frozen Dessert, Chocolate Fudge
    Flavor
  ½ cup, 130 calories, 8 grams fat
  Note: Made with sugar and corn syrup.

Nabisco's Oreos Cookies n' Cream, Vanilla *or*
    Chocolate Flavored Ice Cream
  ⅓ cup, 130 calories, 7 grams fat

Regular Fudgsicle Fudge Pops
  One 1.75-fluidounce bar, 70 calories, 1 gram fat
  Note: Made with sugar and corn syrup.

Three Musketeers Ice Cream Bars, Chocolate
  One 2-ounce bar, 140 calories, 8 grams fat
  Note: Made with sugar and coconut oil.

Weight Watchers Grand Collection Neapolitan Premium
    Ice Cream, Vanilla, Chocolate and Strawberry Flavor
  1 cup, 220 calories, 6 grams fat
  Note: Made with sugar and corn syrup.

Weight Watchers Vanilla Sandwich Bar
  One sandwich, 150 calories, 3 grams fat
  Note: Made with sugar and corn syrup.

Chocolate Candy, Sugar Free

Estee Sugar-Free Milk Chocolate Bar *or*
   Estee Sugar-Free Fruit & Nut Bar
   One .18-ounce square, 30 calories, 2 grams fat
   Note: Made with sorbitol. One bar equals 420 calories
      and 28 grams of fat.

Estee Sugar-Free Crunch Bar
   One .18-ounce square, 22.5 calories, 1.5 grams fat
   Note: Made with sorbitol. One bar equals 315 calories
      and 21 grams of fat.

Estee Sugar-Free Milk Almond Bar
   One .18-ounce square, 30 calories, 2.5 grams fat
   Note: Made with sorbitol. One bar equals 420 calories
      and 35 grams of fat.

Estee Sugar-Free Fruit & Nut Mix, Assorted Chocolate
   Flavored Covered Nuts and Raisins
   4 candies, 35 calories, 2 grams fat
   Note: One box equals 630 calories and 36 grams of
      fat.

Estee Sugar-Free Peanut Butter Cups
   One .27-ounce candy, 40 calories, 3 grams fat
   Note: Made with palm kernel oil and soybean, palm,
      rapeseed, and cottonseed partially hydrogenated
      vegetable oils. One box equals 480 calories and 36
      grams of fat.

Fi-bar, Strawberry with Chocolate Yogurt Coating
   One 1-ounce bar, 99 calories, 3.5 grams fat
   Note: Made with fructose and palm kernel oil.

Chocolate Candy Made with Sugar

Baby Ruth
  2.2-ounce candy bar, 300 calories, 13 grams fat
  Note: To bring this into the calorie/fat range, you may
    eat ¾ bar for 225 calories and 9.75 grams of fat.
  Made with tropical oils.

Butterfinger
  2.1-ounce bar, 280 calories, 12 grams fat
  Note: To bring this into the calorie/fat range, you may
    eat ¾ bar for 210 calories and 9 grams of fat.

Cadbury's Caramello
  5-ounce bar, 700 calories, 35 grams fat
  Note: To bring this into the calorie-fat range, you may
    eat ⅕ bar (1 square) for 140 calories and 7 grams of fat.

Cadbury's Dairy Milk, Milk Chocolate, *or* Cadbury's Fruit
  & Nut, Milk Chocolate, Raisins and Almonds *or*
  Cadbury's Roast Almond, Milk Chocolate and Whole
  Almonds
  5-ounce bar, 750 calories, 40 grams fat
  Note: To bring this into the calorie/fat range, you may
    eat ⅕ bar (1 square) for 150 calories and 8 grams
    of fat.

Cadbury's Krisp
  5-ounce bar, 750 calories, 35 grams fat
  Note: To bring this into the calorie/fat range, you may
    eat ⅕ bar (1 square) for 150 calories and 7 grams of fat.

Hershey's BarNone, "The Chocolate Lover's Bar"
  One 1.5-ounce bar, 240 calories, 14 grams fat
  Note: To bring this into the calorie/fat range, you may
    eat ½ bar for 120 calories and 7 grams fat. Made
    with refined palm kernel oil.

Hershey's Big Block Milk Chocolate
2.8-ounce bar, 440 calories, 24 grams fat
Note: To bring this into the calorie/fat range, you may
eat 1/3 bar for 145 calories and 8 grams of fat.

Hershey's Fifth Avenue
1.8-ounce bar, 250 calories, 11 grams fat
Note: To bring this into the calorie/fat range, you may
eat 3/4 bar for 187.5 calories and 8.25 grams of fat.

Hershey's Krackel Big Block
2.6-ounce bar, 400 calories, 22 grams fat
Note: To bring this into the calorie/fat range, you may
eat 1/3 bar for 132 calories and 7.25 grams of fat.

Hershey's Milk Chocolate Kisses
1.46-ounce package, 9 kisses, 220 calories, 13 grams
fat
Note: To bring this into the calorie/fat range, you may
eat 7 kisses for 170 calories and 10 grams of fat.

Hershey's Milk Chocolate With Almonds
1.55-ounce bar, 250 calories, 15 grams fat
Note: To bring this into the calorie/fat range, you may
eat 1/2 bar for 125 calories and 7.5 grams of fat.

Hershey's Mr. Goodbar
1.85-ounce bar, 300 calories, 20 grams fat
Note: To bring this into the calorie/fat range, you may
eat 1/2 bar for 150 calories and 10 grams of fat.

Hershey's Rolo, Chewy Caramels in Milk Chocolate
1.16-ounce package, 6 pieces, 160 calories, 7 grams
fat
Note: This is already within the calorie/fat range; however, this product contains the tropical oil partially
hydrogenated palm kernel oil.

Hershey's Skor
1.4-ounce bar, 220 calories, 14 grams fat
Note: To bring this into the calorie/fat range, you may eat ½ bar for 110 calories and 7 grams of fat.

Hershey's Symphony Creamy Milk Chocolate
1.4-ounce bar, 220 calories, 13 grams fat
Note: To bring this into the calorie/fat range, you may eat ¾ bar for 165 calories and 9.75 grams of fat.

Hershey's Symphony Creamy Milk Chocolate With Almonds and Toffee Chips
1.4-ounce bar, 220 calories, 14 grams fat
Note: To bring this into the calorie/fat range, you may eat ½ bar for 110 calories and 7 grams of fat.

Kit Kat
1.625-ounce bar, 250 calories, 13 grams fat
Note: To bring this into the calorie/fat range, you may eat ¾ bar for 187.5 calories and 9.75 grams of fat. Made with refined palm kernel oil.

M & M's Plain
1.69-ounce package, 240 calories, 10 grams fat
Note: This is in the calorie/fat range—enjoy!

M & M's Peanut
1.74-ounce package, 250 calories, 13 grams fat
Note: To bring this into the calorie/fat range, you may eat ¾ package for 187.5 calories and 9.75 grams fat.

Mars Bar
1.76-ounce bar, 240 calories, 11 grams fat
Note: To bring this into the calorie/fat range, you may eat ¾ bar for 180 calories and 8.25 grams of fat.

Milky Way
    2.24-ounce bar, 290 calories, 11 grams fat
    Note: To bring this into the calorie/fat range, you may eat ¾ bar for 217.5 calories and 8.25 grams of fat.

Reese's Crunchy Peanut Butter Cups *or*
    Reese's Milk Chocolate Peanut Butter Cups
    1.8-ounce package, 2 cups, 280 calories, 17 grams fat
    Note: To bring this into the calorie/fat range, you may eat 1 cup for 140 calories and 8.5 grams of fat.

Reese's Pieces
    1.95-ounce package, 270 calories, 11 grams fat
    Note: To bring this into the calorie/fat range, you may eat ½ package for 135 calories and 5.5 grams of fat.

Snickers
    2.16-ounce bar, 290 calories, 14 grams fat
    Note: To bring this into the calorie/fat range, you may eat ½ bar for 145 calories and 7 grams of fat.

Three Musketeers
    2.13-ounce bar, 260 calories, 9 grams fat
    Note: To bring this into the calorie/fat range, you may eat ¾ bar for 195 calories and 6.75 grams of fat.

Tiger's Milk Nutrition Bar
    1.4-ounce bar, 160 calories, 6 grams fat
    Note: This is a carob-coated bar, made with corn syrup and brown sugar. One bar equals 1 serving.

Twix
    1.71-ounce package, 2 bars, 260 calories, 14 grams fat
    Note: To bring this into the calorie/fat range, you may eat 1 bar for 130 calories and 7 grams of fat.

"Meal Replacement" Chocolate-Flavor Bars and Drinks

These are not recommended as a substitute for a healthy, balanced, low-calorie diet which utilizes normal foods. However, since many people are drawn (I know I was) to these foods—they appear to be painless ways to eat chocolate candy and still lose weight—they are listed here. The manufacturers have fortified these bars and drinks with vitamins and minerals to meet 10 to 35 percent of the RDA for protein, vitamin A, vitamin C, thiamine (B_1), riboflavin (B_2), niacin, calcium, iron, vitamin D, vitamin E, vitamin B_6, folic acid, vitamin B_{12}, phosphorus, iodine, magnesium, zinc, and copper. One exception is the Pillsbury "figurines 100" Diet Bar—to receive the 25 percent RDA, you must eat two diet bars and drink an eight-ounce glass of skim milk. Much of the RDA is fulfilled from drinking the milk!

Carnation "Slender Diet Meal Bars For
   Weight Control," Chocolate Flavor
   One 1-ounce bar, 135 calories, 7 grams fat
   Note: The first ingredient listed is sugar; it also contains palm oils. One box equals 1,080 calories and 56 grams of fat.

Pillsbury "figurines 100" Diet Bars,
   Natural Chocolate Flavor
   One .75-ounce bar, 100 calories, 5 grams fat
   Note: Made with sugar, cornstarch, and hydrogenated cottonseed and soybean oils. One box equals 800 calories and 40 grams of fat.

Sego from Pet "Lite Liquid Diet Meal for
   Weight Control," Chocolate Flavor
   One 10-fluidounce can, 150 calories, 3 grams fat

Note: Made with sodium saccharin and partially hydrogenated cottonseed oil.

Sego from Pet "Liquid Diet Meal for
  Weight Control," Very Chocolate Flavor
  One 10-fluidounce can, 225 calories, 1 gram fat
  Note: Made with corn syrup and partially hydrogenated cottonseed oil.

Slim Fast Chocolate Flavor Nutrition Bars
  One 1.25-ounce bar, 150 calories, 7 grams fat
  Note: One box equals 2,250 calories and 105 grams of fat. Made with invert sugar, sucrose, and corn syrup; may contain palm kernel oil.

Chocolate Milk, Sugar Free, Hot and Cold

Alba '77 Shake Mix, Chocolate Flavor
  One serving prepared, 70 calories, 1 gram fat
  Note: This is a cold chocolate mix, made with ice and ice water in a blender. Made with partially hydrogenated coconut oil and corn syrup.

Carnation Instant Breakfast, No Sugar Added, Chocolate
  One serving, prepared as directed with 8 ounces low-fat milk, 190 calories, 6 grams fat
  Note: Lower in calories and fat if prepared with skim milk. Contains 25 to 50 percent of the RDA for vitamins and minerals when prepared with milk. Made with NutraSweet.

Carnation Sugar-Free Hot Cocoa Mix, Rich Chocolate Flavor
  One serving prepared, 50 calories, less than 1 gram fat
  Note: Made with NutraSweet brand sweetener.

Estee Reduced Calorie Hot Cocoa Mix
One serving prepared, 50 calories, 0 grams fat
Note: Made with fructose and NutraSweet.

General Foods International Coffees, Sugar Free Suisse Mocha, Swiss Style Instant Coffee Beverage
One 6-fluidounce serving, 30 calories, 2 grams fat
Note: First listed ingredient is hydrogenated coconut oil. Made with NutraSweet brand sweetener. The suggested serving size is rather small, and if you have a larger cup of coffee, your calorie and fat counts will increase.

MJB Sugar-Free Fudge Mocha Chocolate Flavor Instant Coffee Beverage
One 6-fluidounce serving, 40 calories, 2 grams fat
Note: Made with hydrogenated coconut oil and NutraSweet brand sweetener. The suggested serving size is rather small, and if you have a larger cup of coffee, your calorie and fat counts will increase.

Olvatine's Hot Cocoa Mix, Sugar Free Mint
One serving prepared, 40 calories, 1 gram fat
Note: Made with partially hydrogenated tropical oils and NutraSweet brand sweetener.

Swiss Miss Sugar-Free Hot Cocoa Mix
One serving prepared, 50 calories, 1 gram fat
Note: This is prepared with hot water. Made with NutraSweet brand sweetener and partially hydrogenated soybean oil.

Weight Watchers Chocolate Fudge Artificially Flavored Shake Mix
One serving prepared, 70 calories, 1 gram fat
Note: This is prepared with ice and ice water in a blender. Made with partially hydrogenated coconut and soybean oils and NutraSweet brand sweetener.

Weight Watchers Hot Cocoa Mix, Milk Chocolate Flavor
  One serving prepared, 60 calories, 0 grams fat
  Note: This is prepared with hot water. Made with
  NutraSweet.

Chocolate Milk and
Coffees Made with Sugar

Carnation Hot Cocoa Mix, Rich Chocolate Flavor
  One serving prepared, 110 calories, 1 gram fat

General Foods International Coffees,
    Double Dutch Chocolate
  One serving prepared, 50 calories, 2 grams fat

Hills Bros. Old Fashioned Hot Cocoa Mix
  One serving prepared, 110 calories, 2 grams fat
  Note: Made with hydrogenated coconut oil.

Nestle Quik Chocolate Milk
  1 cup, 230 calories, 9 grams fat
  Note: This is prepared chocolate milk, found in the
  dairy case of the grocery store.

Chocolate Pudding
and Mousse, Sugar Free

D-Zerta Reduced Calorie Pudding,
    Chocolate Artificial Flavor
  ½ cup, prepared as directed, 60 calories, 0 grams fat
  Note: Made with cornstarch (first ingredient) and
  NutraSweet.

Featherweight Artificially Flavored
    Chocolate Pudding & Pie Filling
  ½ cup, prepared as directed with skim milk, 60 calories, 0 grams fat

Note: Made with modified cornstarch and NutraSweet brand sweetener.

Jello Sugar Free Cook 'n Serve Chocolate
    Flavor Pudding and Pie Filling
    ½ cup, prepared as directed, 90 calories, 3 grams fat
    Note: Requires cooking and heating of NutraSweet. Made with cornstarch and NutraSweet brand sweetener.

Jello Sugar Free Instant Pudding and
    Pie Filling, Chocolate Flavor
    ½ cup, prepared as directed, 90 calories, 3 grams fat
    Made with Nutrasweet.

Sans Sucre de Paris Sugar Free Chocolate Mousse
    ½ cup, prepared as directed with skim milk, 75 calories, 3 grams fat
    Note: Made with coconut and palm kernel oils and NutraSweet brand sweetener.

Sweet 'n Low Chocolate Custard Mix
    ½ cup, prepared as directed, 70 calories, 1 gram fat
    Note: Made with sodium saccharin.

Weight Watchers Chocolate Flavor Mousse
    ½ cup, prepared as directed with skim milk, 60 calories, 3 grams fat
    Note: Made with hydrogenated coconut oil and NutraSweet.

Chocolate Pudding and Mousse Made with Sugar

Del Monte Chocolate Fudge Pudding, Pudding Cup
    One 5-ounce cup, 190 calories, 6 grams fat
    Note: Made with sugar syrup.

Jell-O Brand Chocolate Mousse Pie
One serving (¹⁄₁₆ 8-inch-round pie), 125 calories, 7.5 grams fat

Jell-O Brand Instant Pudding & Pie Filling, Chocolate Fudge Flavor
One ½-cup serving, prepared as directed with whole milk, 180 calories, 5 grams fat; prepared with skim milk, 150 calories, 2 grams fat

Jell-O Chocolate Pudding Snacks
One 4-ounce serving, 170 calories, 6 grams fat
Note: Made with coconut and palm kernel oils.

Jell-O Rich & Lucious Mousse
One ½-cup serving, prepared as directed with whole milk, 150 calories, 6 grams fat, prepared with skim milk, 120 calories, 3 grams fat
Note: Made with hydrogenated palm kernel oil.

Royal Instant Pudding and Pie Filling, Chocolate Flavor
One ½-cup serving, prepared as directed with whole milk, 150 calories, 6 grams fat; prepared with skim milk, 160 calories, 1 gram fat

Royal Pudding and Pie Filling, Chocolate Flavor
One ½-cup serving, prepared as directed with whole milk, 180 calories, 4 grams fat; prepared with skim milk, 150 calories, 1 gram fat

Sara Lee Chocolate Mousse
1 ounce (¹⁄₂₀ package), 100 calories, 7 grams fat
Note: Made with tropical oils.

Swiss Miss Chocolate Pudding Snacks
One 4-ounce serving, 180 calories, 6 grams fat
Note: May contain partially hydrogenated coconut oil.

Toujé Dutch Chocolate Dessert
One 5-ounce serving, 130 calories, 2 grams fat

Weight Watchers Instant Pudding, Chocolate Flavor
One ½-cup serving, prepared as directed with skim
milk, 90 calories, 1 gram fat
Note: Made with sugar.

Miscellaneous Sugar-Free
Chocolate Snacks

Estee Chocolate Cake Mix
One 8-ounce serving (¹⁄₁₀ cake), 100 calories, 3 grams
fat
Note: Made with fructose.

Estee Fudge Cookies
1 cookie, .23-ounce, 30 calories, 1 gram fat
Note: Made with fructose.

Estee Reduced Calorie Brownie Mix, Double Rich Fudge
One 2-by-2-inch square, 45 calories, 2 grams fat
Note: Made with fructose.

Estee Reduced Calorie Chocolate Syrup, Syrup & Topping
1 tablespoon, 15 calories, 0 grams fat
Note: Made with saccharin.

Estee Sugar Free Chocolate Creme Filled Wafers
One wafer, 20 calories, 1 gram fat
Note: Made with sorbitol and soybean oil.

Lite Munchies Rich Chocolate Snack Chips
One ½-ounce bag, 60 calories, 2 grams fat
Note: Contains no wheat or other grains. Made with
NutraSweet, dried chocolate milk, and soybean oil.

"Skinny Munchies" by Skinny Haven, Chocolate
Fudge Flavored Crispy Chocolate Treats
One ½-ounce bag, 66 calories, 2 grams fat

Note: These are chocolate-flavored chips made with corn meal, sunflower oil, fructose, and cocoa.

Sweet 'n Low Brand Chocolate Flavored Cake Mix
One Serving (1½-inch-diameter round or ¹⁄₁₂ cake baked in 8-inch square pan), 90 calories, 2 grams fat
Note: This is prepared by adding water and baking. Made with sorbitol. One cake equals 1,080 calories and 24 grams of fat.

Sweet 'n Low Brand Chocolate Flavored
Frosting & Fudge Topping Mix
One serving,* 30 calories, 2 grams fat
Note: This is prepared by adding water and mixing with a beater.
*The frosting is prepared with more water than the fudge topping, and therefore the suggested serving sizes for the frosting and the fudge topping are different. For the frosting, the serving is 1½ teaspoons, and for the fudge topping, the suggested serving size is 1 teaspoon.

Chocolate Cakes, Cookies, and Toppings Made with Sugar

Betty Crocker Angel Food Chocolate Flavor
Cake Mix, Contains No Fat or Cholesterol
One serving (⅛ 10-by-4-inch tube pan), 225 calories, 0 grams fat.

Betty Crocker Creamy Deluxe Chocolate Flavored Frosting
1.3 ounces (approximately 2½ tablespoons), 170 calories, 8 grams of fat
Note: Made with beef tallow and/or palm oil, as well as sugar and corn syrup.

Betty Crocker Fudge Brownie Mix
    One 2-by-2-inch square, 130 calories, 5 grams fat
    Note: May contain tropical oils.

Betty Crocker MicroRave Devils Food Cake Mix
    With Chocolate Flavored Frosting
    One serving (1/10 frosted cake prepared in pan provided with mix), 180 calories, 9.6 grams fat
    Note: May have tropical oils or animal fat.

Betty Crocker MicroRave Frosted Brownie Mix
    One serving (1/8 prepared and frosted brownies made in pan provided with mix), 180 calories, 7 grams fat
    Note: May contain tropical oils.

Betty Crocker MicroRave Fudge Brownies
    One serving (1/8 prepared brownies made in pan provided with mix, 140 calories, 5 grams fat
    Note: May contain tropical oils.

Betty Crocker Super Moist Chocolate Flavored Cake Mix
    One serving (1/15 13-by-9-by-2-inch cake, 210 calories, 10 grams fat

Duncan Hines Chewy Recipe Fudge Brownie Mix
    One 2-by-2-inch square, 130 calories, 5 grams fat

Duncan Hines Chocolate Gourmet Turtle Brownie Mix
    One 2-by-2-inch square, 220 calories, 9 grams fat
    Note: Made with partially hydrogenated coconut oil.

Duncan Hines Original Double Fudge Brownie Mix
    One 2-by-2-inch piece, 160 calories, 7 grams fat

Duncan Hines Traditions Devil's Food Cake Mix
    One serving (1/18 9-by-13-inch cake), 190 calories, 10 grams fat

Hostess Devil's Food Cupcakes
    One cupcake, 185 calories, 6 grams fat

Hostess Ding Dongs
    One cake, 187 calories, 10.5 grams fat
    Note: To bring this into the calorie/fat range, you have
        to bring the fat count to 10 grams or less. This
        means eating 95 percent of 1 cake.

Hostess Ho Hos
    One cake, 118 calories, 6 grams fat

Nabisco Chips Ahoy
    Two cookies, 130 calories, 6 grams fat

Nabisco Fudge Oreos
    Two cookies, 150 calories, 8 grams fat

Nabisco Oreo Cookies
    Three cookies, 140 calories, 6 grams fat

Nabisco Striped Chips Ahoy
    Two cookies, 150 calories, 8 grams fat

Nabisco Striped Chocolate Chip Cookie's 'n Fudge
    Three cookies, 150 calories, 8 grams fat

Pepperidge Farm brownie cookies
    One cookie, 168 calories, 9 grams fat

Pillsbury Best Natural Chocolate Flavored
        Chocolate Chip Cookies
    Three 2¾-inch cookies, 200 calories, 10 grams fat
    Note: This is premade cookie dough, found in the
        refrigerated section of the grocery store.

Pillsbury Best Natural Chocolate Flavored
        Chocolate-Chocolate Chip Cookies
    Two 2½-inch cookies, 140 calories, 6 grams fat
    Note: This is premade cookie dough, found in the
        refrigerated section of the grocery store. Made with
        hydrogenated coconut oil.

Pillsbury Deluxe Fudge Brownie Mix
  One 2-inch square, 150 calories, 7 grams fat

Pillsbury Microwave Cake Mix and Frosting, Chocolate
    Cake Mix and Natural Chocolate Fudge Flavor Frosting
  One serving ($\frac{1}{16}$ 7-inch round cake, 150 calories,
    8.5 grams fat

Pillsbury Microwave Fudge Brownie Mix
  One 2½-by-2½-inch square, 180 calories, 9 grams
    fat

Pillsbury Natural Chocolate Fudge Flavor Frosting
    Supreme
  ⅓ ounces (approximately 2½ tablespoons), 150 calo-
    ries, 6 grams fat

Pillsbury Plus Pudding in the Mix Devils Food Cake Mix
  One 2-inch square, 180 calories, 9.5 grams fat
  Note: May contain hydrogenated animal fat.

Pillsbury Ready to Microwave Fudge Brownies
    with Chocolate Flavored Chips
  One 1.5-ounce brownie, 180 calories, 9 grams fat
  Note: Found in the refrigerated section of the grocery
    store. Made with sugar and chocolate liqueur.

Sara Lee Chocolate Fudge Cake Snacks
  One cake, 1.6 ounces, 190 calories, 10 grams fat
  Note: Made with sugar and corn syrup.

Sara Lee Fudge Brownie Pie Snacks
  One half of one 2.125-ounce brownie, 140 calories, 7
    grams fat
  Note: This is a prepared dessert found in the freezer
    section of the grocery store. Made with sugar and
    corn syrup.

Smuckers Chocolate Fudge Topping
2 tablespoons, 130 calories, 1 gram fat
Note: Made with corn syrup, high-fructose corn syrup, and sugar.

Thin Mints, Girl Scout Cookies
One cookie, 40 calories, 2 grams fat

Weight Watchers Chocolate Brownie
One 1.25-ounce brownie, 100 calories, 4 grams fat
Note: This is a prepared dessert found in the freezer section of the grocery store. Made with saccharin, fructose, and sugar.

Weight Watchers Chocolate Cake
One 2.5-ounce cake, 180 calories, 5 grams fat
Note: This is a prepared dessert found in the freezer section of the grocery store. Made with sugar, fructose, high-fructose corn syrup, and saccharin.

Weight Watchers German Chocolate Cake
One 2.5-ounce cake, 200 calories, 8 grams fat
Note: This is a prepared dessert found in the freezer section of the grocery store. Made with sugar and saccharin.

Chocolate-Flavor Cereals Made with Sugar

General Mills Cocoa Puffs
1 ounce with ½ cup skim milk, 150 calories, 1 gram fat
Note: Made with coconut oil.

Kellogg's Cocoa Krispies
1 ounce with ½ cup skim milk, 150 calories, 0 grams fat
Note: May contain coconut oil.

Post Cocoa Pebbles Crisp Sweetened Cereal With Real
Cocoa
1 ounce with ½ cup skim milk, 150 calories, 1 gram
fat
Note: Made with hydrogenated coconut oil and/or
palm kernel oil.

Ralston Chocolate Chip Artificial Flavor Cookie-Crisp
1 ounce with ½ cup skim milk, 150 calories, 1 gram fat
Note: Made with coconut oil.

Chocolate-Flavor Breakfast and Granola Bars, Made with Sugar

Carnation Chocolate Chip Breakfast Bars
One 1.45-ounce bar, 200 calories, 11 grams fat
Note: To bring this into the calorie/fat range, you may
have ¾ bar for 150 calories and 8.25 grams of fat
May contain tropical oils.

Kellogg's Pop Tarts, Frosted Chocolate Fudge Flavor
One pastry, 200 calories, 4 grams fat
Note: Sweetened with sugar, dextrose, and corn syrup.

Kellogg's Rice Krispies Bars, Chocolate Chip Flavor
One 1-ounce bar, 120 calories, 4 grams fat
Note: May contain tropical oils.

Kudos Chocolate and Granola Snack, Nutty Fudge Flavor
One 1.3-ounce bar, 190 calories, 12 grams fat
Note: To bring this into the calorie/fat range, you may
have ¾ bar for 142.5 calories and 9 grams of fat.

Quaker Granola Dipps, Caramel Nut Flavor
One 1.1-ounce bar, 140 calories, 6 grams fat
Note: May contain tropical oils. Made with chocolate
liqueur.

Quaker Granola Dipps, Chocolate Chip Flavor
    One 1-ounce bar, 140 calories, 6 grams fat
    Note: Made with chocolate liqueur.

Quaker Granola Dipps, Chocolate Fudge Flavor
    One 1.1-ounce bar, 160 calories, 8 grams fat
    Note: Made with chocolate liqueur.

Quaker Granola Dipps, Peanut Butter Chocolate Chip
    Flavor
    One 1.15-ounce bar, 170 calories, 11 grams fat
    Note: To bring this into the calorie/fat range, you may
        have ¾ bar for 127.5 calories and 8.25 grams of fat.
        Made with chocolate liqueur.

Bibliography

Aronson, V. "Magic Sandwiches." *Health*.

Bland, J.B., ed. *Medical Applications of Clinical Nutrition.* New Canaan, Connecticut: Keats Publishing, Inc., 1983.

"Calorie Control Commentary." No author listed. Atlanta: Calorie Control Council, Spring 1989.

Chin, M.L. "Sweet Fears: Swapping Sugar and Calories for Headaches and Cancer?" *Longevity*.

"Chocolate: The All-Consuming Passion." No author listed. *Current Health*.

"Chocolate Bars." No author listed. *Consumer Reports*.

"Curb the Cola." No author listed. *Longevity*.

Frank, E., and Rubenstein, D. "Frequency of Sexual Dysfunction in Normal Couples." *New England Journal of Medicine*.

Friedrich, J.A. *The Pre-Menstrual Solution: How To Tame the Shrew in You.* San Jose: Arrow Press, 1987.

Hayton, B. "Keeping Stress at Bay the Nutritious Way." *Current Health*.

Herbert, W. "Mind-Altering Sweetener? Bittersweet Victory for Sugar Substitute." *Science News*.

Hunter, B.T. "Aspartame: Pro and Con." *Consumer Research*.

Katz, S. "Chemistry's New Sweets." *Technology Review* (1983): 81.

Kritchevsky, D. *Nutrition Research,* March 1989, as reported in *News,* Chocolate Manufacturers Association of the USA, June 1988.

Pauly, D., Resener, M., et al. "Sweet Dreams for Searle." *Newsweek.*

Pennington, J.A.T., and Church, H.N. *Food Values of Portions Commonly Used.* New York: Harper & Row, Publishers, Inc., 1985.

Schuman, M., Gitlin, M.J., and Fairbanks, L. "Sweets, Chocolate, and Atypical Depressive Traits." *Journal of Nervous and Mental Disease.*

Skoogfors, L. "A Bitter Dispute over NutraSweet's Safety." *Businessweek.*

Stone, J. "Life-Styles of the Rich and Creamy." *Discover:* 81–83.

Tooley, J.A. "Oh, Chocolate." *U.S. News & World Report:* 75.

Virtue, D.L., and Freidrich, J.A. *Eat, Sleep and Be Sexy.* Nashville: Envision Videotapes, 1989.

————. *The Yo-Yo Syndrome Diet.* New York: Harper & Row, Publishers, Inc., 1989.

Wellness Letter. Berkeley: University of California, School of Public Health, April 1989.

COOKBOOKS

Cooking for every lifestyle

☐ **BETTER HOMES AND GARDENS NEW COOKBOOK**
(26766 • $6.95)
The Cookbook used in more American kitchens than any other is
now better than ever! Over 1200 delicious recipes plus meal
planning guides and menus, and hundreds of recipes for appliances,
easy meals and great new entertainment ideas.

☐ **THE FANNIE FARMER COOKBOOK** (25915 • $6.95)
A heritage of good cooking for a new generation of cooks. Since
1896 when Fannie Merritt Farmer published the first BOSTON
COOKING-SCHOOL COOKBOOK, it has been the culinary bible
for generations of American women. The original has been continu-
ally updated by her heirs, and, now, 86 years and 12 editions later,
THE FANNIE FARMER COOKBOOK is better than ever.

Special Cooking Needs
☐ **COOKING WITHOUT A GRAIN OF SALT** by J. Bagg
(27241 • $4.50)
☐ **RECIPES FOR DIABETICS** (27150 • $4.95)

And don't miss these other Bantam Cookbooks

☐ **MICROWAVE COOKERY** by Deacon (26254 • $4.95)
☐ **CROCKERY COOKERY** by Hoffman (25604 • $4.95)
☐ **BETTY CROCKER'S COOKBOOK, 6th Ed.**
by Betty Crocker (26660 • $6.95)
☐ **THE FRENCH CHEF COOKBOOK**
by Child (26434 • $5.95)
☐ **THE COMPLEAT I HATE TO COOK BOOK**
by Bracken (27130 • $4.95)
☐ **COUNTRY BAKING: SIMPLE HOME BAKING WITH
WHOLESOME GRAINS** by Haedrich
(Hardcover) (07048 • $22.95)

INVEST IN THE POWERS OF YOUR MIND
WITH SUBLIMINAL SELF-HELP TAPES
FROM BANTAM AUDIO PUBLISHING

The Bantam Audio Self-Help series, produced by Audio Activation, combines sophisticated psychological techniques of behavior modification with subliminal stimulation to help you get what you want out of life.

For Women

- [ ] 45004 **SLIM FOREVER** $8.95
- [ ] 45035 **STOP SMOKING FOREVER** $8.95
- [ ] 45041 **STRESS-FREE FOREVER** $8.95
- [ ] 45172 **DEVELOP A PERFECT MEMORY** $8.95
- [ ] 45022 **POSITIVELY CHANGE YOUR LIFE** $8.95
- [ ] 45106 **GET A GOOD NIGHT'S SLEEP...**
  EVERY NIGHT $7.95
- [ ] 45094 **IMPROVE YOUR CONCENTRATION** $7.95
- [ ] 45112 **AWAKEN YOUR SENSUALITY** $7.95

For Men

- [ ] 45005 **SLIM FOREVER** $8.95
- [ ] 45036 **STOP SMOKING FOREVER** $8.95
- [ ] 45042 **STRESS-FREE FOREVER** $8.95
- [ ] 45173 **DEVELOP A PERFECT MEMORY** $8.95
- [ ] 45023 **POSITIVELY CHANGE YOUR LIFE** $8.95
- [ ] 45107 **GET A GOOD NIGHT'S SLEEP...**
  EVERY NIGHT $7.95
- [ ] 45095 **IMPROVE YOUR CONCENTRATION** $7.95
- [ ] 45113 **AWAKEN YOUR SENSUALITY** $7.95

Look for them at your local bookstore or use this handy page for ordering:

Bantam Books, Dept. BAP4, 414 East Golf Road, Des Plaines, IL 60016

Please send me ____ copies of the tapes the items I have checked. I am enclosing $_____(please add $2.00 to cover postage and handling). Send check or money order, no cash or C.O.D.s please. (Tape offer good in USA only.)

Mr/Ms _____

Address _____

City/State _____ Zip _____

BAP4—9/90

Please allow four to six weeks for delivery.
Prices and availability subject to change without notice.